MARY KNEW

Großvater nahm er sich ganz anders vor, der musste Stellung nehmen, weshalb er den Hochzeitstag wieder einmal vergessen hatte und schwören, dass er in dieser Nacht der Weihnachtsgans nicht wieder einen gebratenen Flügel stehlen würde. Und als der Weihnachtsmann fragte, ob Großvater zum Fällen der Tanne etwa Großmutters bestes Küchenmesser benutzt hatte, rief ich voller Verzweiflung: „Opa, ich habe nicht gepetzt." Großvater strich mir über die Wange und sagte gereizt: „Lass mal Kind. Ich weiß längst, wer dem Weihnachtsmann solche Dinge in die Ohren tutet." Von meinen Verfehlungen im Laufe des Jahres schien der Weihnachtsmann keinen blassen Schimmer zu haben, denn im Gegensatz zum Großvater bekam ich nie etwas mit der Rute. Aber noch lieber als zu mir war der Weihnachtsmann zu Großmutter. Er zählte alle ihre guten Taten auf, ließ sich von ihr mehrere Gedichte aufsagen und nahm sie dafür jedes Mal in die Arme. Als er sie nach dem dritten Gedicht auf die Stirn küsste, sagte Großvater: „Nun reicht es, Gustav". Ich war sehr froh, endlich einmal den Vornamen des Weihnachtsmannes zu hören, aber in meinem Aufsatz habe ich ihn nicht notiert, denn Frau Pingel behauptete, dass Weihnachtsmänner weder einen Vor- noch Nachnamen haben.

Und in den Geschichten, die sie uns in den letzten Stunden vor den Weihnachtsferien vorlas, wurde immer lieblich gesungen. Bei uns ließen die Großeltern die Leute aus dem Radio singen und spielten gleich nach der Bescherung Skat. Denn jedes Mal, nachdem der Weihnachtsmann gegangen war, kam kurz darauf der Briefträger ganz zufällig bei uns vorbei. „Nein, so eine Überraschung", rief die Großmutter, und der Großvater brubbelte „Ja, ja" vor sich hin. Großmutter raffte die bestickte Decke vom runden Tisch, und Großvater füllte drei Gläser mit Korn, während der Briefträger die Karten mischte und uns allen „Frohe Weihnacht" wünschte. Und während ich meine Geschenke auspackte, mit Genuss zwei Schokoladenweihnachtsmännern den Kopf abbiss und Theaterstücke in der nagelneuen Puppenstube aufführte, hörte ich vom runden Tisch die Fäuste von Großvater, Großmutter und vom Briefträger lieblich auf den Tisch trommeln, und dazu klimperten die winzigen Berge aus silberfarbenen Pfennigen. „Darfst dir noch eine Apfelsine holen", sagte Großmutter. Ich genoss es, die Nase in das Päckchen zu stecken, das Tante Elsbeth aus Lübeck geschickt hatte. Nichts duftete Weihnachten so lieblich wie der Schuhkarton von Tante Elsbeth, in dem Orangen, Backpulver, Kaffee und Seife nebeneinander lagen. Und dieser einmalige Duft überführte Großmutter auch der Lüge. Ich glaubte ihr nicht, wenn sie mir einen Tag vor dem Fest vorjammerte, diesmal hat Tante Elsbeth gar nix geschickt. Ich hatte den Duft längst erschnüffelt und hätte mit Sicherheit sagen können, in welcher Kommode es diesmal versteckt war.

In der Nacht des Heiligabend schlief es sich gut im klammen schweren Federbett, weil mein Schlafanzug zuvor in der Ofenröhre kräftig gewärmt wurde, und es duftete noch immer im ganzen Haus nach Bratäpfeln, Tannengrün und dem Schuhkarton von Tante Elsbeth.

Und ich träumte himmlisch. Mit beiden Fäusten trommelte der Weihnachtsmann an Frau Pingels Tür. Er trug kurze Hosen, einen schwarzen Zylinder und überreichte ihr einen riesigen Umschlag. „Ein Geschenk für mich?", fragte Frau Pingel begeistert. Der Weihnachtsmann nickte und sagte: „Das ist ein Aufsatz von einem Kind mit dem grünsten Tannenbaum von der ganzen Welt." Sie musste ihn lesen, nachdem er ihr alle ihre Rotstifte abgenommen hatte, und dann ließ der Weihnachtsmann Frau Pingel ganz eiskalt stehen.

MARY KNEW

A DEFENSE OF THE VIRGIN BIRTH OF CHRIST

———⧖———

RICHARD LARRY BROOKS, II.

Xulon Press
2301 Lucien Way #415
Maitland, FL 32751
407.339.4217
www.xulonpress.com

© 2022 by Richard Larry Brooks, II.

All rights reserved solely by the author. The author guarantees all contents are original and do not infringe upon the legal rights of any other person or work. No part of this book may be reproduced in any form without the permission of the author.

Due to the changing nature of the Internet, if there are any web addresses, links, or URLs included in this manuscript, these may have been altered and may no longer be accessible. The views and opinions shared in this book belong solely to the author and do not necessarily reflect those of the publisher. The publisher therefore disclaims responsibility for the views or opinions expressed within the work.

Unless otherwise indicated, Scripture quotations taken from the King James Version (KJV) –*public domain.*

Paperback ISBN-13: 978-1-6628-5298-5
Ebook ISBN-13: 978-1-6628-5299-2

Dedication

———∝———

This book is dedicated to my greatest gifts: Leigh, Ally, and Logan. Each has been an immeasurable source of inspiration and encouragement to me.
All my love and thanks.

I would also like to thank my mother, Vera Brooks Anderson, for instilling in me the love and appreciation for the Christmas story. Mom, I hope this work encourages others to love this holiday as much as you have encouraged me.

To those who will take time to read and consider the contents of this work: "The LORD bless you and keep you; The LORD make His face shine upon you, And be gracious to you; The LORD lift up His countenance upon you, And give you peace."
(Numbers 6:24–26)

Contents

Introduction xi
Chapter 1: Admitting Bias 1
Chapter 2: Isaiah's Prophecy Examined 7
Chapter 3: Redemption Promised through Eve 19
Chapter 4: Persecutor Turned Preacher 29
Chapter 5: The Unlikely Disciple 37
Chapter 6: That You May Know with Certainty 59
Chapter 7: Mary Knew 75
Chapter 8: Jesus' Words and Works 87
Chapter 9: Jesus' Resurrection 103
Chapter 10: Conclusion 117
About the Author 127
Notes 129

Introduction

The Focus of this Work

The Christmas holiday is enjoyed around the world. In fact, it is one of the few days when armies will lay down their weapons to enjoy a momentary application of the words once whispered by angels to a group of terrified shepherds, "On earth peace, good will toward men" (**Luke 2:14**). Whether individuals are people of the Christian faith or not, it seems the majority have a fondness for this observance that commemorates the birth of a little Jewish boy born in an obscure village, in a country barely recognizable on the world map in His day.

The story as told today is one filled with wonderful pageantry even while it is told against the backdrop of a humble stable filled with livestock and straw. It is with joy many believers turn out each year to watch children depict the cast of characters described by Matthew and Luke in their gospels. Attendees are reminded of the angels who heralded the birth of the child along with the wise men who came bearing gifts and the shepherds showing up unannounced for a surprise visit. Mary and Joseph, all the while are sitting in reverence marveling over the miracle entrusted to them. Yes, it is a beautiful story retold by thousands of congregations both small and large all over the world annually.

While the story is often depicted with such conviction and certainty by congregations, there are elements of the account that have long been and continue to be debated. Scholars, students, and others with varied opinions have and continue to weigh in on this narrative. Often, these thinkers try to undermine the most foundational tenets of the story. One such tenet is commonly referred to as the virgin birth or the more scholarly, miraculous conception event. This detail, though regularly debated today, has been the subject of much discussion throughout the centuries.

Early church authority Origen Adamantius (AD 185–254) in his *Contra Celsum* argued against a heretical tale circulating in his day that the infant Jesus was the product of an affair between Mary, the child's mother, and a Roman soldier.[1] The tale was probably offered as means to undermine the miraculous conception origin of Jesus as told by the early church because of the church's growing influence on the Roman Empire, which was beginning to upset the status quo of religious expression within the empire.

While the debate of Jesus' origin remains unsettled to many people, it must be acknowledged that the virgin birth theme is the central tenet to the nativity story. It is my opinion that, more importantly, the miraculous conception is the very bedrock on which the rest of Jesus' biography rests and will be considered throughout this work.

Why this Work?

It is my intent, after careful consideration of many of the traditions and assumptions surrounding the nativity story, to offer a thoughtful defense of the biblical position of Jesus' conception. The reason for such consideration is to lend needed support to the traditions celebrated by Christians for centuries. Many of these traditions, and beliefs, are under attack today.[2] Many individuals and institutions who claim critical enlightenment have attacked people of faith for their beliefs and have marginalized the group as being nothing more than foolish. But is there an ulterior, underlying reason for the assault? Is there a legitimate reason many individuals no longer trust the Bible as the authoritative source for revelation into this and other subjects? You should consider why so many people today have decided to reject Jesus and doubt the biblical testimony that has shaped western civilization for thousands of years. Has evidence been discovered which has debunked biblical testimony or otherwise proven it false? The answer simply is no. Contrary to the opinions of unbelievers, there is no source of information that has proven the scriptures as unreliable. As a matter of fact, the so-called evidence many use to disprove the claims of Scripture is far more untrustworthy and takes far more imagination to believe than the biblical record.[3]

What has changed regarding the validity of Scripture is simply interpretation. It must be understood that human interpretation stems from perspective. Perspective is nurtured from the experiences logged in the heart and mind of the interpreter. Scripture explains the unregenerate heart of man to be wicked (**Jer. 17.9**), and that wickedness takes pleasure in sin (**Prov. 2.12–15**). Jesus is recorded as predicting there will come a time when sin will become rampant and the hearts of many shall grow cold toward truth (**Matt. 24.12**). Given current opinions and events, it seems this might be the time to which Jesus points.

Today, there is growing hostility to anything that validates the testimony of Scripture.[4] As you look around at the modern state of affairs within the United States and parts abroad, we are left with certainty that we are indeed facing perilous times as are described by the apostle Paul when he wrote, "evil men and seducers shall wax worse and worse, deceiving, and being deceived" (**2 Tim. 3:13**). These seducers also embody the words of the Prophet Isaiah who warned against such efforts to undermine the authority of God's standards when he wrote,

> Woe unto them that call evil good, and good evil;
> that put darkness for light, and light for darkness;
> that put bitter for sweet, and sweet for bitter!

Which justify the wicked for reward, and take away the righteousness of the righteous from him!

Therefore as the fire devoureth the stubble, and the flame consumeth the chaff, so their root shall be as rottenness, and their blossom shall go up as dust: because they have cast away the law of the Lord of hosts, and despised the word of the Holy One of Israel. (**Isa. 5.20, 23, 24**)

If there ever was a time when the Word of God was abandoned by western society, this certainly seems to be that time. The apostle Paul seems to rightly describe the participants found in today's decadence as "blasphemers . . . despisers of those that are good . . . lovers of pleasure more than lovers of God" (**2 Tim. 3:2–4** author's paraphrase). These people seem to look for ways to ignore and even undermine the authority of God at every turn (**Rom. 1:30**). It seems such behavior has always resulted in the execution of judgement by God. Jesus himself predicted that such behavior in the latter times would parallel that perpetrated by the wicked just prior to the judgement escaped only by Noah and his family in the antediluvian world (**Matt. 24:37–39**). According to Paul it is not that people are ignorant of God's words, they simply choose to ignore what He is communicating (**2 Tim. 3:8**), as is the case with the miraculous conception account described in the both the Old and New Testaments.

While pages could be filled addressing a number of subjects explaining why people should embrace the Bible as truth, I have purposefully limited the discussion here to address the virgin birth account. Why arrive at such a decision? I feel that if this subject can be logically defended and evidence is provided to substantiate the matter, other points of contention that people often point to in the biblical record become mute.[5] Further, if the miraculous conception can be logically supported, this should result in a crisis of faith for anyone faced with the evidence. One must either accept the evidence presented as truth and believe or reject the evidence and intentionally deny. If you accept the evidence presented, you must then decide whether you can trust the Bible as a whole and if so, will you then submit yourself to the authority of Jesus which leads to salvation (**Matt. 28:18**)? Ultimately, this is the dilemma which motivates all who argue against the reliability of the scriptural record. Some may claim scholarly intent but ultimately the debate centers around a very simple question asked by Jesus late in His ministry, "But whom say ye that I am?" (**Mark 8:29**).

Numerous individuals today embrace anti-authoritarian views, searching for any reason to delegitimize any claim of Jesus exercising authority over them. They look for reasons to reject Jesus because they don't want to acknowledge His sovereignty as judge. If they find reason to doubt Him, they mistakenly believe they're accountability to Him is extinguished. This is why many argue

Introduction

for the so-called historical interpretation of Jesus, which dismisses any claims of His deity. However, the testimonies of Scripture and the historical record, along with common sense will prove Jesus was much more than a mere man as will be explored in the following discussion.

You are being asked to keep an open mind and to give real consideration to the following evidence as it relates to the virgin birth. By the end, hopefully you will be as convinced as I am of the historicity of this blessed event.

1
Admitting a Traditional, Conservative Bias

It is Christ Himself, not the Bible, who is the true Word of God. The Bible, read in the right spirit and with the guidance of good teachers, will bring us to Him.—C.S. Lewis

I admit I approach the Scriptures with a blatant conservative bias. As discussed in the Introduction, interpretation is a matter of perspective. Perspective is defined by experience, often accumulated over a lifetime. While I own the conservative influence afforded me by my seminary training, the greater influence is owed to my personal experience. The God of the Bible has repeatedly intervened in my life. Thus, God has proven to me not only His existence outside the pages of the Bible but also His interest in the affairs of my life. It would stand to reason if God is interested in the life of this one individual, He must also be interested in the affairs of mankind as a whole or so it would seem. This line of reasoning supports the position of Scripture that God genuinely cares for His creation and because of His plan to redeem it, He has and will continue to intervene throughout the annals of time.

The greatest example of God's intervention is the sending of His Son, Jesus to redeem humanity through the miraculous conception event. As discussed earlier, there are scores of individuals who want to acknowledge Jesus as anything but divine. There is great effort exerted by thinkers hoping to provide evidence that Christians have saddled Jesus with false claims of divinity.[6] In their minds, these are claims Jesus never intended for himself. The argument can be seen in the following.

One need only perform a quick Google search of Jesus' virgin birth to find article after article that provides ample reason to doubt the very details depicted by the New Testament regarding the particulars surrounding Jesus' origins.[7] There are many voices such as that of Bart D. Ehrman of the University of South Carolina who have rejected notions such as the virgin birth and other elements of Jesus' life, based on his self-identification as a proclaimed agnostic.[8]

You must always understand interpretation is colored by the lens through which the question is viewed. If an individual is predisposed to have doubt or find fault with a statement, in this case from Scripture, he will without doubt find an argument or evidence to support his predetermined position.

Many readers may remember the 1970's hit country music single by John Conlee entitled "Rose Colored Glasses." Within the chorus of the song, there are lyrics which apply perfectly to the statement made in the preceding paragraph. The lyrics read as follows, "But these rose colored glasses that I'm looking through show only the beauty 'cause they hide all the truth." The point being simply that people see only what they want to see. This certainly is the case with many skeptical views calling into question the life and meaning of Jesus' birth and very existence.

But it is also understood that the individual who is arguing and promoting the biblical interpretation of Jesus' birth narrative or any other such biblically presented account is also using his own pair of glasses to arrive at his point of view. The lens through which he offers interpretation is called faith. While many would reject faith as being a vehicle by which rational interpretation can be ascertained, there is biblical support which argues this approach as being the only way of truly understanding the observable world and can only be rightly received by a regenerated heart and mind. The writer of the Book of Hebrews offers, "By faith we understand that the entire universe was formed at God's command, that what we now see did not come from anything that can be seen"

(**Heb. 11:3 NLT**). What the author of the statement is saying is that not everything can be explained by the limited understanding of man. He is saying one must always leave room for the probability of divine interference into the world.

It is here you should pause to consider the emphasis placed upon how the person of faith is to allow his faith to transform him. This transformation is not only to occur in the heart but also in the head of the believer. Often skeptics will argue Christians use faith as a crutch to deny what is plainly observed in the natural world. But notice the words of the apostle Paul who writes "Do not be conformed to this world, but be transformed by the renewal of your mind, that by testing you may discern what is the will of God, what is good and acceptable and perfect" (**Rom. 12:2 ESV**). The point being that true interpretation and understanding can only be obtained with the help of the Divine who unclouds the ability of man to rightly process information. The inference here being that the fall of man into sin not only marred his heart but impaired his mind as well (**Rom. 5:12–21**). Wow, what a truly amazing statement concerning man's perspective! All the understanding he hopes to gain through educational and intellectual pursuits will end in his ultimate deception without the help of the Divine (**John 16:8–11**).

It must also be stated that in today's modern world doubt or skepticism is seen as virtue. Skepticism is often applauded by the masses when it is applied to anything that hints of tradition and/or convention, especially where morality is concerned.[9] An "anything goes" approach is usually adopted by those who hope to dismiss institution or to redefine what is morally acceptable. Skepticism can be seen in the lack of maintaining a baseline of socially agreed upon behavior. Ultimately, what is being argued through skepticism is basically the law of entropy, the process of things breaking down without outside maintenance. Such a breakdown is the result of skepticism towards social morality. This process is observed in the natural world.[10] It is also the case with interpretation. If we doubt simply to doubt without proper justification, chaos results, and there remain no absolutes on which to rest.

For clarity purposes, I believe unequivocally the Bible represents God's complete and true communication to man. I am convinced God is capable of communicating His expectations of morality or anything else through the very medium He provided man, the written word.

Further, God is quite able to protect and preserve His message through the centuries to present it to the modern reader in words he can understand. It is simply illogical to assume God, who is understood to be omnipotent and omniscient, does not have the ability to communicate effectively His intent. Without getting into a scholarly discussion on the varied opinions of biblical hermeneutics, I intend to apply common sense conservative interpretation to the discussion of Jesus' origin and leave the scholarly debate to those with loftier theological pedigrees.

I am reminded of advice I once received years ago from noted biblical scholar Dr. Harold Willmington of Liberty University who said, "When the common sense of Scripture makes good sense, seek no other sense." Thank you, Dr. Willmington, for providing such a wonderful tool for interpretation.

Now that the baseline for the proceeding discussion has been established, it is time to turn attention to the evidence provided those hoping to better understand the virgin birth event. The first piece of evidence to be explored is the prophecy written by Isaiah some seven centuries before the event unfolded in Bethlehem.

2

Isaiah's Prophecy

---—⚭———

Therefore the Lord himself shall give you a sign;
Behold, a virgin shall conceive, and bear a son,
and shall call his name Immanuel.
(Isaiah 7:14)

This verse written by the prophet Isaiah seems very clear when read at face value, at least by the English reader. The prophet explains that a virgin will conceive and bear a son. For millennia Christians have read this verse and understood it to mean that a female who had not engaged in sexual intercourse would become pregnant by supernatural means and bear a son. However, many modern academics argue that this traditional understanding is wrong.[11] They argue that such an understanding reflects ignorance of the true interpretation of the language used by Isaiah. This argument centers on the meaning of the word *virgin* used by Isaiah and has been debated among academics for years.

Bart Ehrman in his online blog provides a current example of the debate writing, "Sometimes the word [virgin] simply means 'young woman.' And that is definitely what the original Hebrew of Isaiah 7:14 says, where the Hebrew word for 'young woman' (*alma*) is used, rather than the word for 'woman who has never had sex' (*bethulah*)."[12] Ehrman's emphatic conclusion has left many of the faithful questioning whether their collective understanding and faith in Jesus as the fulfillment of the prophecy is justifiable. Unfortunately, Ehrman and others like him have used their opinions and their academic pedigrees to undermine many of the very tenets of traditional Christian faith and have encouraged many in today's world to abandon common sense interpretation and ultimately, moral virtue as defined by the Bible because of their insistence in proving Jesus was nothing more than a traveling showman.[13]

While Ehrman and others would refute this claim and insist their intent is to foster nothing more than critical thinking and to encourage the pursuit of intellectual honesty when it comes to biblical interpretation, the truth is they are doing a disservice to the original intent of the Bible writers. Original intent meaning the reason behind why the writers wrote their works the way they did. While some may argue we can never know what motivated these men to write their contributions to the Bible, it seems very obvious to me that biblical writers wrote to encourage readers to faith; the term *faith* meaning dependence upon God to honor His commitment to man. This observance is very plain if the Bible is read from an objective perspective with no preconceived intent. However, Ehrman and most of academia would have students examine the biblical text with the goal of discrediting its intent.

According to Ehrman, Isaiah is simply saying that a young mother will bear a son and his name will mean "God is with us." His conclusion being that those who translated the Hebrew *alma* into English simply used the wrong word in translation, which conveyed a misguided notion to readers of the verse. While Ehrman's hermeneutical approach appears to be sound at first glance, there are reasons why the verse is interpreted as claiming a *virgin* shall give birth to a son. The following are a couple of observances which support the "virgin" interpretation.

LANGUAGE EXAMINED

לָכֵן יִתֵּן אֲדֹנָי הוּא לָכֶם אוֹת הִנֵּה הָעַלְמָה הָרָה וְיֹלֶדֶת בֵּן

alam
young girl

וְקָרָאת שְׁמוֹ עִמָּנוּ אֵל:
(Isaiah 7:14, Great Isaiah Scroll, Qumran)

This verse has been pulled directly from the Great Isaiah Scroll, which was found by Bedouin shepherds in

1947. It, along with many others, was discovered in a cave at Qumran just north of the Dead Sea in Israel. Without going into an exhaustive discussion on the history of the find and the subsequent conversation as to its value for modern biblical interpretation, it is generally agreed by scholars that the Dead Sea Scrolls discovery provides some of the oldest extant copies of the Hebrew Bible. In some cases, the find represents manuscripts almost a thousand years older than known copies collected before the discovery.[14]

The Great Isaiah Scroll is generally accepted to have been copied between the first and second centuries BC based on writing samples from the work.[15] The actual Book of Isaiah is thought to have been written around the seventh century B.C.[16] This means that the Great Isaiah Scroll was copied about five or six centuries after the actual writing of the book by Isaiah. While the actual book has been lost to time, early copies such as the Isaiah scroll can better represent the original contents of the book. This line of reasoning argues that the earlier the copy the less likely it is to be corrupted by edits or redactions to support later views or opinions of a reader. Thus, the earlier copy allows us a better understanding of what the writer was actually saying when he completed his work.

There are minor differences within the Great Isaiah Scroll and today's Masoretic Text (Hebrew Bible), as seen in copies such as the Leningrad and Aleppo Codices.

These codices are ancient copies of the Hebrew Bible. These differences are mostly grammatical.[17] This is a wonderful fact to discover as these codices are thought to be 1,000 years younger than the Great Isaiah Scroll. This illustrates how careful the scribes were who copied these texts to accurately represent the original document. In the case of this discussion, it provides you confidence that Isaiah's use of the word *alma* was not a later revision. You are reading what is thought to be the intended message from Isaiah's pen.

Now that there is ample evidence that Isaiah's choice term of *alma* was intentional, it is time to examine how the word is used by Isaiah. *Alma* can mean "young woman" as pointed out by Erhman. However, a term such as *alma* has to be taken within the context in which it was written. When I attended seminary years ago, we had a Greek professor, Gregory Stephens, who constantly reminded students that in the case of translation and/or interpretation, "context is always king." With Professor Stephens in mind, I wish to apply this simple rule to the interpretation of the term *alma*.

According to the Kohlenberger/Mounce Concise Hebrew-Aramaic Dictionary of the Old Testament, *alma* is used seven times in the Old Testament.[18] Each time the word is used, the context of the usage denotes an implied understanding that the referenced "young girl" is a virgin. In Exodus 2:8 for example, *alma* is used to identify Moses' sister who followed him after he was placed in the ark, or basket, made by his mother to see where the water would take him. She was young and would have been understood by the reader to have been a virgin because of her youth. Also in Genesis 24:43 Abraham's servant describes Rebekah, the daughter of Bethuel, soon to be wife of Isaac, as an *alma*, which is translated "virgin." Rebekah too would have been understood by the reader to have been young and a virgin, which were the characteristics desired for the potential wife candidate for Isaac. More to the point, the writer of Genesis not only implies Rebekah's virginity through his word choice but directly states in the text she was a virgin (**Gen. 24.16**). Therefore, *alma* is directly clarified by the context of Scripture as representing the characteristic of virginity.

Erhman is using the same tactic the serpent used on Eve in Eden. He seems to be employing a half truth. Yes, *alma* can mean "young girl" as stated by Erhman, but the term has greater implied meaning being that the "young girl" was a virgin. The English term *maiden* is similar in that it once carried the implied meaning that a young girl was a virgin because of her youth. It is my opinion that Erhman is no doubt stirring controversy simply for the sake of publicity, not that there really exists a misunderstanding of the term.

It is also my opinion that for a modern scholar to insist that *alma* only means "young girl" in Hebrew is simply perpetrating a fraud upon those who seek his opinion. It is the height of arrogance to insist that a modern critical opinion carries more weight than the clear intent of the original writer. The original reader considering Isaiah's work in 7:14 would have understood that the "young girl or maid" to which Isaiah was referring would have been chaste or untouched by a man in sexual terms because of her youth. If virginity wasn't the implied condition from which the birth resulted, what would have been so special about a young mother having a child? Thousands of young Jewish mothers were having babies every day with no special attention given. But in the case of Immanuel's mother, something special was clearly implied by Isaiah's mention.

There is yet another strong piece of evidence that supports Isaiah's intended meaning of the term. This piece of evidence was considered and held in high regard by many of the greatest Jewish scholars of history along with many in the early church. This next piece of evidence is known as the Septuagint.

The Septuagint Translation

For those unfamiliar with the Septuagint, a brief biographical sketch is necessary. The Septuagint is the Greek translation of the Hebrew Scriptures. The work is said to have commenced in the third century BC with work on the Torah. These first five books of the Old Testament would have been completed over the next several years, adding more of the Hebrew books to the collection over time.[19]

The reason for the translation seems clear enough. There were a large number of Jewish communities spread throughout the Middle East at the time which had assimilated into the Hellenistic culture with a large population in Alexandria, Egypt, where Greek became the primary language spoken by the group. Over time, these Greek speaking Jewish communities desired a translation of their sacred texts which could be utilized for religious and moral learning. So, the Greek King of Egypt, Ptolemy II Philadelphus, commissioned the work.[20]

Beyond the needs of the Jewish community, Ptolemy had commissioned the work because of his desire to include the Jewish Torah into the Library of Alexandria. The library is described as housing thousands of manuscripts representing various cultures and thinkers in its day. It is described as possibly containing texts and information now lost to history as the library was eventually destroyed. The Septuagint gained popularity within the Jewish population and is referenced widely by Paul in his New Testament writings. Further, the translation was used by other early Christian writers such as church father Irenaeus and was even read by Jesus as recorded in Luke's gospel describing his work as Messiah.[21]

Now, on to its significance within this discussion: the very purpose of the Septuagint translation was to produce a reliable representation of the Hebrew scriptures for

Greek readers. While there are minor differences in the copies of the Septuagint and the Great Isaiah Scroll found at Qumran, most are linguistic which have little bearing on implied understanding. The two works are similar in dating as both are thought to have been copied in the first or second centuries BC. This is significant because it demonstrates the term found in both Isaiah sources as *alma,* was used intentionally and was not a mistake at the hand of a scribe or a translator. The term was not found in one source and not the other. Therefore, the Isaiah Septuagint translators translated the Hebrew word *alma* into the Greek text by using the word *parthenos,* both of which represent virginity.[22] More specific, these translators used the Greek term *parthenos,* which offers a very similar meaning of the Hebrew *alma*, which is translated as "maid" with the implication of implied virginity. This is not only the case in Isaiah but also in the description of Rebekah in Genesis 24:43 as well.

The implication of the translation unfortunately is either overlooked or dismissed by researchers. However, here it will be offered as evidence of the reliability of the translation and its implied meaning. The men selected to provide the Septuagint translation were among the best linguists and students of the Tanakh, or Hebrew Bible, of the day.[23] It is my opinion that the arrogance of modern scholars who dismiss or minimize the clear intent of the words the original writers chose for the translation is just short of insanity. The Septuagint translators knew the implied meaning behind the terms and believed the words they used for translation would communicate clearly to a Jewish reader that the referenced "maid" described by Isaiah would be taken to mean a young girl who had not engaged in physical intimacy with a man. Again, this is the same use of the term as used by Moses to communicate the youth and purity of Isaac's bride in Genesis 24:43. A Jewish reader would have very clearly understood the meaning behind the terms used for translation.

One other possibility should be considered before this chapter comes to a close. There are those who insist that *alma* should be translated simply as "young girl" as has been discussed. However, it must be asked why the Septuagint translators chose the "virgin" translation of the term. It would be thought that out of the multiplicity of scholars working on the translation, red flags would have been raised if consensus on translation for the term could not have been reached. While this argument is somewhat outside of the consensus of modern scholarship on the subject, is it possible the text the translators were working from used the more consistently translated term for "virgin," which is *bethulah*? It is unclear if this could be the case as there are no surviving copies of the original Hebrew scroll of Isaiah which can be considered as dating to the time of its translation into the Greek Septuagint. Or, might we possibly believe the words of the Apostle Peter who penned "but holy men of God spake as they were moved by the Holy Ghost?" (**2 Peter**

1.21). Perhaps God provided special insight to the translators as to how best to translate the term. The point being that God is very capable of getting across His message to the reader of Scripture.

Now that clear consideration has been given to the Isaiah text which is questioned by many who are critical of the claims of Jesus' virgin birth, focus will be turned to other references within sacred Scripture that imply a miraculous conception event for the birth of the Messiah, or Christ.

3

Redemption Promised through Eve

---—∞—---

*And I will put enmity between thee and the woman,
and between thy seed and her seed; it shall bruise
thy head, and thou shalt bruise his heel.
(Genesis 3:15, KJV)*

While I expect that many will disagree with the conclusion I've offered in the proceeding chapter, it seems rather clear Isaiah's prophecy points to a virgin birth for the promised son, who would be a sign to wayward Israel. The biblical record seems to perfectly corroborate Isaiah's prophecy as one considers the larger testimony of Scripture. From the earliest record of the inspired writings, this idea of miraculous conception seems to have been implied long before Isaiah picked up his pen.

Genesis 3:15 is known in many circles as the "Protoevangelium," or the first gospel, for its promise of a deliverer who would defeat mankind's original tempter, the serpent from the garden of Eden.[24] Within the early pages of Genesis, the virgin birth narrative seems to be first floated by God. In God's declaration of condemnation upon the three participants involved in the fall episode, He seems to suggest the offspring from the woman, independent of her husband, would be responsible for ultimately destroying the serpent for his role in subjecting mankind to death.

While biologists will argue God's declaration must include Adam as the catalyst who enabled Eve to procreate, the language indicates a supernatural occurrence for the birth of mankind's future avenger. "I will put enmity between you (the serpent) and the woman, and between your off spring (the serpent) and hers; he will crush your head, and you will strike his heel" (**Gen. 3:15 NIV**).

Note, the two individuals being addressed in this text are not the man and the woman, nor the man and the serpent. The two individuals in this declaration are the woman and the serpent. Yes indeed, the woman and the serpent! The declaration is preceded by God directly announcing judgement upon the serpent in verse fourteen of the chapter. The transition between verses fourteen and fifteen is uninterrupted as a continued pronouncement of judgement upon the serpent. God specifically announces that the offspring of the woman would be responsible for the serpent's demise.

Some readers may dismiss this observation to simply misguided inference or to a slip of the pen by the author of Genesis, Moses. I admit, I am no expert on the Hebrew language and I confesses my use of various study tools which contribute to my observations. However from my elementary deduction, no other time in Scripture is a woman referred to as being able to sow seed of procuration (HB-עֶרֶז, GK-zera) on her own. Typically a woman is explained as conceiving or giving birth to seed (HB-עֶרָז, GK-zara) as is identified in Leviticus chapter twelve. Observe the transliteration of Genesis 3:15 provided in the following:

LANGUAGE EXAMINED

וְאֵיבָה ׀ אָשִׁית בֵּינְךָ וּבֵין הָאִשָּׁה וּבֵין
זַרְעֲךָ וּבֵין זַרְעָהּ הוּא יְשׁוּפְךָ רֹאשׁ וְאַתָּה
zera   zera
seed   seed
תְּשׁוּפֶנּוּ עָקֵב: ס
(Genesis 3:15, Septuagint LXX)

You should understand I am not saying Eve conceived of her own accord. However, from a human perspective, this may seem to be true and this is what the language of Genesis would seem to suggest. But Luke tells us the

Holy Spirit was responsible for providing the necessary ingredient to begin the conception process within Eve which resulted in the birth of the Redeemer promised in the early pages of Genesis (**Luke 1:35**).

Significance

The implications of the Holy Spirit being the impetus for the birth of the Savior are monumental but when actually considered, makes perfect sense as far as the biblical narrative goes. Consider the magnitude of what has occurred in the fall of man event: the human race has become permanently corrupted by sin. While many today do not consider there being a big difference in the experience of the first man and woman after tangling with sin, it seems those who have considered the subject thoughtfully have a very different opinion.[25]

There are those who suggest the fall of man had drastic and immediate implications on the first couple.[26] Today, people pay little attention to sin, as they see it has no immediate effect on their lives. But I maintain the current state of man's existence wasn't always as he knows it today. Consider, some have suggested the likeness referred to in Genesis as being shared by Adam and God has nothing to do with bodily characteristics but with luminosity.[27] Yes that is right, some theologians believe man once glowed. Talk about a drastic and definite change. As far out as this sounds if it were once true, it would indeed be a colossal change in the very appearance of man, one which would certainly have been noticed by Adam after his fall thus giving evidence to the fact that something was wrong and had indeed changed the immediate nature of man.

I remember partaking in discussions while in seminary as to whether Jesus performed miracles out of His ability as God or as the perfect man (**Phil. 2:6–9**). It was suggested Jesus' ability to do miracles, such as walk on water and turning water into wine, were accomplished from His perfect human nature not as miracles conjured from His deity.[28] The implication being that man once had far greater skills and abilities in his initial created state than he currently possesses in his fallen state today; the assumption being that those skills and abilities were lost during his fall or following after having been mutated by sin (**Rom. 5:12–21**).

Even ancient writers seemed to believe there was more to the fall than mere nuisance, which had far greater implications for the lives of the first couple. In the ancient works, the Books of Adam and Eve, the author seems to paint a very bleak tragedy occurring from the fall event.[29] The writer in the early pages of the work pens, "when Adam looked at his flesh which was altered, he wept bitterly, he and Eve, over what they had done" (**1 Adam and Eve 4:2**). While the student of Scripture wouldn't consider these words with the same weight as he would those recorded in the inspired cannon of Scripture, he can get a sense that earlier readers of the ancient text were left with some impression that the fall of man carried far greater implications than are commonly believed today.

All this has been said to provide substantiation for the following conclusion. Charles Darwin's ideas of inheritance may have some limited application here. Darwin writes, "from the strong principle of inheritance, any selected variety will tend to propagate its new and modified form."[30] This statement seems to in fact explain very well the mutated inheritance that Adam has handed down to each of his progeny. While many may disagree, I believe man's existence today is limited by his inherited sin condition. In fact, even the most healthy among men is actually broken and is dying because of the effects of this inherited sin condition. While men may work hard to reverse or limit the effects of this inherited condition, the effort is essentially useless as all men die just as Adam died from this mutated state.

Men continue to pass on the seeds of Adam's mutation to their offspring making their offspring just as broken. The significance here is that man cannot fix his condition as it is interwoven into his DNA. If man is to receive a fix for his broken condition, the remedy would have to be placed into existence from an outside agent. It is here that God enters into the equation. God interjected Christ into the bloodline of men allowing Him to become the remedy for the sin condition (**Gal. 4:4**). However, Christ's conception was independent of the seed from his fathers, thus giving credibility to the possibility that man's sin condition is transferred through the male Y chromosome.

The idea of Christ as the Redeemer is then simplistically defined as one who has a remedy or fix for the inherited brokenness resulting from sin. This fix would come from a divine source as described earlier, not of the offspring of man. We can trace the moment of God's intervention providing the fix historically in the writings of Luke who penned the words, "The Holy Ghost will come upon thee (Mary), and the power of the Highest shall overshadow thee; therefore also that holy thing which shall be born of thee shall be called the Son of God" (**Luke 1:35**).

Why Virginity?

Some may wonder if virginity was a necessary prerequisite for the mother of the Redeemer, though it seems rather obvious that surely it was. Why was it necessary? Could God have impregnated a woman who had already given birth from the seed of man with the Redeemer? The answer in short is yes. He most certainly could have done so. He can do anything (**Mark 10:27**). However, knowing naysayers would have asserted that the birth of the Redeemer was nothing more than the result of another man-made pregnancy, as many do today regardless of the evidence. God chose to do the miraculous. He chose to leave man out of the equation entirely. He chose to wrap the Redeemer within the womb of a simple, virgin peasant girl who willingly humbled herself to His will. As for a potential father, sin would need a sacrifice without the inherited blemish of sin. Adam's corrupted seed would play no role in the birth of Jesus. Therefore, Mary became the only human ingredient necessary.

Finally, it is interesting that Mary is spoken to by the angel without the witness of anyone else attesting to the conversation. The reason this is interesting is that her testimony is the sole grounds for the virgin birth narrative in the New Testament. This coming at a time when women's testimonies were not admissible in court proceedings or in matters of a legal nature. This demonstrates that God likes to color outside the lines. He does not have to bend to the conventions of His creation. The ways of God are not the ways of a man (**Isa. 55:8–9**). God doesn't need a man or men to justify His works. He is God. He can do whatever He deems necessary.

The Protoevangelium is certainly interesting to consider as it provides support to the theory that the virgin birth was the means which God intended to use for placing His Redeemer into the world of man from the very beginning as recorded in Genesis. While there are people who will reject many aspects behind this idea and while more time could be spent defending it, attention will now be turned to the testimony of a few of the pillars of Christianity on the matter of virgin birth. The first position to be considered from the group will be that of the man responsible for writing much of the New Testament canon—the man also responsible for shaping much of orthodox Christian theology—the apostle Paul.

4

Persecutor Turned Preacher

———∝———

But when the fulness of the time was come, God sent forth his Son, made of a woman, made under the law.
(Galatians 4:4)

It is interesting how readily it is forgotten the lengths to which New Testament writers went to accurately record the details of the gospel narrative. There is no greater testimony to this fact than what is recorded by the apostle Paul in 1 Corinthians 15 when he writes, "For I delivered unto you first of all that which I also received" (**1 Cor. 15:3**). This statement declares the intent of the apostle to provide an accurate account of the details surrounding the faith he had placed in the risen Christ. Dr. Gary Habermas of Liberty University suggests this statement may have in fact been pointing to an early Christian creed learned by believers to convey the truths of the gospel message. Habermas writes that the creed links the historical life of Jesus with eyewitnesses who could attest to the authenticity of the events surrounding his life.[31] Paul specifically points out to the Corinthian church there were many who had witnessed Jesus' life who were still living and available to testify to the accuracy of his message. Paul's personal quest for the truth surrounding Jesus should provide us with assurances of his desire to accurately preserve the historical record.

Consider Paul's own record of his quest for details as he writes to the church at Galatia. He penned, "Then after three years I went up to Jerusalem to see Peter, and abode with him fifteen days. But other of the apostles saw I none, save James the Lord's brother" (**Gal. 1:18, 19**). The implications of this meeting are monumental. There would have been no greater eyewitnesses to the life and ministry of Jesus. Peter was Jesus' right hand during His ministry, while James would have witnessed Jesus' life from his early years forward. The information these men potentially passed on helped to provide Paul a foundation on which to build.

By Paul's own account he was a man of learning, a Pharisee by training (**Phil. 3:5**). Luke provides greater description of Paul's education by stating he sat at the feet of Gamaliel, a great Jewish rabbi during Paul's day (**Acts 22:3**).[32] The importance of this discussion is that Paul understood the value of applying clear reasoning to substantiate a position. This is demonstrated by Gamaliel's own words as recorded by Luke in his advice to the council when discussing the fate of imprisoned apostles. He explains, "But if this be of God, ye cannot overthrow it" (**Acts 5:39**). This type of thinking was no doubt embedded into Gamaliel's students as evidenced by Paul in his many writings. On one occasion Paul writes, "whatsoever a man soweth, that shall he also reap" (**Gal. 6:7**). Paul employs rational deduction to arrive at logical conclusions. Clearly this was not a man given to flights of fantasy or mythmaking. If there had been no evidence to support the claims of Christian belief, Paul surely would have seen through the ruse. This applies to the claim of Jesus' miraculous conception.

Many have argued Paul never considered the claims of the virgin birth narrative because the idea was a later construct imposed by Christians to support the idea that Jesus should be regarded as the Deity.[33] However, such claims seem hollow when considered against the evidence recorded by Paul's own words.

First, consider Paul's words as he wrote to the church at Galatia. He penned, "I went up to Jerusalem to see Peter and abode with him fifteen days. But other of the apostles I saw none, save James the Lord's brother" (**Gal. 1:18, 19**). While no one can be sure exactly how many days he spent in conversation with either man individually, the text states he did possibly spend fifteen days listening to details of Jesus' life and ministry. As explained earlier, these details were provided by none other than the best authorities regarding both, Peter and James.

Peter had firsthand details surrounding Christ's ministry. He was there from beginning to end. He would have seen the faces of the five thousand who were fed with the five loaves and two fishes (**Matt. 14:13–21**). He would have heard Jesus call to Lazarus in the tomb (**John 11.1–44**). And, he witnessed the resurrected Christ ascend into heaven (**Acts 1:9–12**). There would have been no greater eyewitness to Jesus' words and work during His ministry.

James likewise would have been an exceptional witness to the life of Jesus. He likely was with Mary and Joseph when they had to leave the caravan and return to Jerusalem to look for Jesus after realizing he was not with the family as they returned to Nazareth (**Luke 2:41–52**). He along with his siblings and mother would have gone to retrieve Jesus from a Galilean synagogue when Jesus first began His ministry (**Mark 3:21**). And while he would not have been there personally, there is no doubt he heard his mother and father recount the circumstances surrounding his older brother's birth more times than he cared to admit. A better witness to these events could not have been produced.

The experience of these two men is what prompted Paul to seek them out as he sought to better understand the backstory of his faith in Christ. It is interesting to consider Paul's account regarding his motives for the meetings with the men. The words translated "to see" by the King James interpreters, in the Greek, is *historeō*. This word is translated by Thayer's Greek-English Lexicon as "to inquire into, examine, investigate."[34] It seems quite logical Paul quizzed the men regarding the particulars of the Jesus tradition. At this time, Paul was new to the faith. However, his education within the rich tradition of Judaism had ingrained within Paul the value of historical tradition. It was to this end that Paul was seeking information. It is here Peter and James began to fill in the story for Paul and to provide the answers to the questions Paul had regarding how it all began and took shape. Like many new believers who would come after him, Paul sought to better understand the events which led up to his conversion and to a greater extent, understand his place in the larger scheme of God's plan for redemption.

Speaking from my experience, I shared this same desire as Paul. I came to know Christ in my teens. At the time, I attended a small independent Baptist church in the community where I was raised in North Georgia. While the services and fellowship were sweet, there was not an overwhelming amount of information that explained the why, how, and when. Those within the congregation were expected simply to believe and that was enough for the small country church. However, I had a desire to know more regarding God and the plan and history for the church, from which I was called to ministry. This led me to attend seminary where I hoped to find answers to my questions.

While some might argue that Paul's discussions with Peter and James never resulted in the apostle learning of the miraculous conception narrative, the evidence seems to suggest otherwise. In Galatians 4:4, Paul explains that God's son was "born of a woman." This reference seems to suggest Paul's belief in a miraculous conception origin for Jesus. Consider Paul's use of the term *born*. The Greek form of the word is *ginomai*. The word means "to come into existence."[35] While some may argue against my impression, it seems Paul is alluding to Christ being born to a woman without the ordinary interaction of an earthly father. Notice his specific reference to the fact that Christ is the Son of God (**Gal. 4:4**). His reference seems to intentionally exclude the necessity of an earthly father. In fact, Paul never seems to reference Joseph, Jesus' earthly father. Therefore if the intent of Paul is as described, he provides belief of the virgin birth in what is accepted as his earliest recorded written correspondence to the Galatian church.

Some may argue my evidence for suggesting that Paul advocates for the virgin birth narrative is flimsy at best. But consider, neither Paul nor any of the other New Testament writers ever argue against the idea. If Paul was indeed on a mission to discover the truth surrounding the fledgling sect and its executed leader, it seems likely that he would have wanted to correct any misinformation undermining its legitimacy. Yet it seems overwhelmingly plausible he passed the idea on to those he influenced, as with Luke, placing his stamp of approval on the doctrine of virgin birth. Paul seems to provide even more legitimacy to the virgin birth account by quoting from what appears to be Luke's gospel where the virgin birth story is recorded within his own correspondence to Timothy (**1 Tim. 5:17–18**). If Paul is quoting Luke and he had problems with Luke's impressions regarding the birth narrative, he surely would have had no problem correcting his traveling companion as he once did Peter (**Gal. 2:11–14**). This is not the case however.

Some would assert that Luke's gospel wasn't available to Paul to quote if critical dates for Paul's death and the completion of Luke's book are accepted as fact. However, Luke's words could be much older than expected by critical scholarship if Paul is indeed quoting them.[36] Perhaps, Paul's death is later than realized. Or perhaps, Luke shared his notes with Paul on occasion or maybe what is witnessed is Luke penning what his teacher, Paul taught him. The simple truth of the matter is that timelines can often be difficult to nail down with certainty.

It is particularly interesting to consider that the writings of Luke probably were an account of what Paul was actually teaching to his sphere of influence. His teachings, including the virgin birth, would form the bedrock on which the infant church would build its creeds and doctrines. It is also with these same teachings that Paul would train those who would come after him in the faith to lead the churches he would leave behind. While consideration is being given to this idea, more on Luke's writing objectives will be examined coming up in this work.

For now, you are encouraged to consider the second person Paul interacted with during his fifteen-day stay in Jerusalem, James. Peter would have been crucial in relaying the historical account of the ministry of Jesus. But James would have been the voice which could have been able to speak directly to questions regarding things such as the virgin birth story and other matters pertaining to Jesus' life before His ministry. James could provide insight into who Jesus was outside of the attention of His ministry.

5

The Unlikely Disciple

---∞---

After that, he was seen of James; then of all the apostles.
(1 Corinthians 15:7)

It is appropriate to consider James the head of the church at Jerusalem with more detail, for James is indeed the most unlikely of candidates for the role of disciple to Jesus. Many who read James' epistle in the New Testament are oblivious to the importance of James other than the obvious information he provides through his written work. Here however, consideration will be given to James' importance for advocating the virgin birth narrative.

James' Influence

James would have been a wonderful resource for learning about Jesus' life before His ministry. His insight into what is sometimes referred to as the historical Jesus would have been second to none.[37] James would have had firsthand knowledge into his brother's life few others could portray.[38] He would have grown up, playing and learning from many of the same people and circumstances as the young Jesus.

As siblings come up, circumstances can either unite or sever the relationships within a family unit. Often, the same event can send siblings on very different paths. It is interesting to consider what appears to be a special relationship between Jesus and James. As Paul points out, Jesus specifically reaches out to James after His resurrection. Paul writes, "After that, he was seen of James; then all the apostles" (**1 Cor. 15:7**). This appearance account seems peculiar at first glance. Why would Jesus make a point to single out James for a special post-resurrection appearance when it seems He didn't reach out to any other of His family members specifically? Speculation is useful to possibly answer this question.

When reading the passages of Mark 6:3 and Matthew 13:55–56 you are introduced to the siblings of Jesus. Mark writes, "Is not this the carpenter, the son of Mary, the brother of James, and Joses, and of Juda, and Simon? and are not his sisters here with us?" (**Mark 6:3**). Whether or not these are step or biological siblings, sharing Mary as mother, is irrelevant to the point being made.[39] However, I am inclined to believe the siblings to be biological. Regardless, it would seem the list may suggest James was the second eldest son of the group. This deduction stems from the practical experience to which I have been exposed. Growing up in the South, any list of siblings usually is presented in descending order from oldest to youngest. If this is the case, leadership of the group would usually fall to the second oldest if something were to have occurred to the eldest son. James may have found himself in this position.

Consider with the death of the father, as is assumed of Joseph, Jesus would have had the responsibility of providing for the family. This expectation is probably the activity in which Jesus toiled for the majority of his adult life. While evidence for this assumption is scarce regarding Jesus, considering the expectation of the average Jewish adult male makes the conclusion most likely probable.[40] The oldest abled male usually provided for the welfare of the family unit in the event of the death or decline of the paternal male. This is why it was important for male progeny to be produced to a family. Work was hard and backs had to be strong in order to provide. Although there are many fanciful stories regarding Jesus' lost years of a possible itinerary abroad, such a possibility seems unlikely at best.[41] It is generally accepted by most mainstream scholars Jesus would have been too busy providing for His family to have had time to achieve little else.

Decidedly, Jesus would have been the primary provider for His family with the loss of Joseph. His adulthood prior to His ministry at the age of approximately thirty, would have been marked by labor most likely as a builder. Again, Mark 6:3 provides clues to substantiate this conclusion. Consider Mark's passage, "Is not this the carpenter?" (**Mark 6:3**). Strong's Greek Dictionary defines the occupation *tekton* as "a craftsman in wood."[42] I have also heard suggestions that Jesus' trade may have also included masonry. Regardless, He would have most likely learned the skills necessary for the trade from Joseph (**Matt. 13:55**) and would have used His skills to make a living for His family. It is also within the realm of probability His brothers would have learned the same woodworking skills from Joseph and labored alongside their older brother, Jesus.

When Jesus announces His ministry, there appears to be a clear break between what is assumed to be His responsibility of providing for the family and His larger work of atonement for mankind. Consider Matthew's words, "From that time Jesus began to preach" (**Matt. 4:17**). Each of the writers of the gospels present Jesus as essentially showing up on the scene with very little background provided before His ministry begins. There is obviously good reason for this as most writers, whether writing about Jesus or any other subject, concentrate on the perceived important material. These writers, as John states, are writing to present Jesus to their readers in hopes they will receive Him as Messiah or Christ (**John 20:31**).

This break would have no doubt left the responsibility for providing for the family to the next male in line, James. It is interesting that on two occasions James is assumedly with other family members trying to intervene for Jesus when His teaching became too controversial for listeners who had gathered to consider His words (**Mark 3:21; Matt. 12:46**). Presumably, James would have become the collective voice of authority for the family and would have likely been dubbed the voice of reason by the family in their quest to rationalize with and for Jesus. It is assumed they hoped Jesus would suspend what the family probably considered a fool's errand of becoming a marked dissident by the Jewish or Roman authorities.

With James stepping into this patriarchal lead for the family, it would have been his duty to take responsibility for the family, which seemed to believe the oldest brother, Jesus, had become mentally unfit (**John 3:21**). However, a remarkable change occurs within the family's attitude towards Jesus and His claims of divine mandate after Jesus' resurrection. Luke records that after Jesus' ascension into heaven, Jesus' brothers could be found praying alongside the apostles, with Mary, His mother and others (**Acts 1:14**). While the New Testament provides the names of the brothers of Jesus as James, Joses, Jude, and Simon (**Matt. 13:55**), only mere speculation can be offered as to the exact number of siblings who were represented at the prayer vigil. However a plurality is described and based upon the collection of their epistles within the New Testament, James and Jude likely constituted the number represented at the vigil, or at least a portion of it.

The question as to why the change of heart about Jesus must be considered. New Testament students will likely know the answer to this about-face by his brothers, at least as it pertains to James. In 1 Corinthians 15, Paul provides the clearest timeline of events immediately following the resurrection of Jesus. In the account Paul provides a list of who interacted with the resurrected Christ (**1 Cor. 15:3–8**). The list seems typically boiler plate as to whom the reader might expect to be listed, except for one name which seems out of place on the list. This is the name of James.

It is interesting that James is singled out for a personal post-resurrection visit by Jesus. Paul writes, "After that, he was seen of James; then of all the apostles" (**1 Cor. 15:7**). From the information provided by the gospel authors, James had not had a change of heart concerning his older brother even up to the point of Jesus' crucifixion. Based on the information provided, James was still an unbeliever regarding Jesus' claims as to being the Messiah or Christ of Israel. Probably more to the point, he may have resented his older brother for leaving the burden of providing for the family upon his shoulders. This is speculation of course, but in any case, James is never accounted among the followers of Jesus or even present at Jesus' crucifixion.

It is quite telling that neither James nor any of Jesus' siblings were represented at His crucifixion. Whether this was out of resentment or embarrassment is simply a guess. Some may argue opportunity was their excuse for this lack of attendance, but we read of John and others standing in the shadows of the cross or at least close enough for Jesus to converse with them (**John 19:25–27**). Nevertheless, none of Jesus' siblings were in attendance. They seemed to have abandoned their older brother. So, why would Jesus have made time to visit with James after His resurrection? It makes sense Jesus would have visited Peter and others among His followers to guide them back to the path of belief after the blow of His death. James was not a wayward follower who may have felt hollow and/or resentful for following what appeared to be nothing more than a waste of time and energy. However, Jesus makes an intentional visit to James. It seems Jesus had plans for His brothers, particularly James and Jude.

According to the early church historian, Eusebius (AD 260–339), Jesus' siblings played roles in the continuance of the gospel and the growth of the church. In his *Historia Ecclesiae,* Eusebius speaks of Jesus' family's continued influence within the church. He can be quoted as using the term *desposyni* to describe the blood relatives of Jesus' family who were chronicled as active participants on the church's attendance roles.[43] Another ancient writer who actually coined the term *despoyni* was Sextus Julius Africanus (AD 160–240) who's usage of the term is preserved by Eusebius in the same work.[44] Both of these early church historians testify to the continued influence Jesus' family played in the development of the early church.

It isn't until after Jesus' resurrection that we witness the family activity within His fledgling movement. The first hint of such is portrayed within Luke's chronicle in Acts 1. Luke writes, "These all continued with one accord in prayer and supplication, with the women, and Mary the mother of Jesus, and with his brethren" (**Acts 1:14**). By the time of the upper room prayer meeting, James and others of Jesus' family were among those waiting for Jesus' promise of the Holy Spirit at His ascension. Paul seems to credit Jesus' appearance to James as the catalyst for James' conversion leading to his eventual ascent to leadership into the church (**1 Cor. 15:7**).

It is interesting to read how Luke explains that the apostles were "together with the women and Mary the mother of Jesus, and his brothers" (**Acts 1:14**). Some would argue the use of the term *delphos,* meaning "brothers," simply means those sharing the same faith. However, the root term in Greek (*delphus*) actually means "of the same womb."[45] It is true the term is used by New Testament writers to designate those born into the family of God and is still used in churches all over the world today to signify Christian brotherhood. One example used within Scripture is Peter using the term in his second epistle to describe the relationship he shared with Paul calling him a "dear brother" (**2 Peter 3:15**). This term is also used by Paul to describe the relationship he forged with Sosthenes to the church at Corinth. (**1 Cor. 1:1**). So, the use of the term to designate Christian fellowship within the confines of the shared faith is legitimate. However, Luke seems to imply something more as he gives account of those huddled in the upper room (**Acts 1:14**).

If the verse is taken out of the context from which it is written, you could justifiably argue that Luke was simply referring to Christ's brothers in the faith as being present during this gathering of early believers. However as Professor Stephens would always point out during seminary, context is king. The two preceding verses penned by Luke specifically name the apostles as being in attendance at the meeting (**Acts 1:12,13**). Luke lists these apostles by name, acknowledging the body of the apostles was absent one member. The member missing is obviously Judas Iscariot, who by this time had committed suicide. The point being made here is that the designated fellowship of apostolic brothers is accounted for and present. The brethren to which Luke is referring in verse 14 is logically to be understood as Jesus' biological brothers. He drives this point home by naming Jesus' mother, Mary, as an attendee and couples her name alongside the phase "his brethren." This would suggest to the casual reader of his text, that Luke was referring to Jesus' blood brothers who were of the house or progeny of Mary, His mother.

There may be some who would further argue the brothers reference could refer to other disciples of Christ who constituted the remaining number of the 120 believers referenced by Luke in the following verse (**Acts 1:15**). But after a careful reading of verse 15, this argument is easily settled. Luke indicates that days may have passed before the events described in verse 15 took place where the reference to the 120 believers is acknowledged by use of the phrase, "In those days." The verses used by Luke earlier to describe the upper room meeting seem to indicate a much smaller and intimate group joined the apostles directly following Jesus' ascension. Luke seems to describe this tattered group as those who were closest to Jesus, an inner circle might be the best way to describe the group.

It is logical to place James as part of this group referred to as "his (Jesus') brethren" (**Acts 1:14**). Again for clarity, I believe the group to be Jesus' biological siblings. Paul's testimony in his letter to the Corinthians leads us to infer James' attendance within the group because of his personal post-resurrection visit by Jesus (**1 Cor. 15:7**). But who else might have been in the number which is identified as being plural? It seems logical to speculate Jesus' brother Jude or Judas (**Matt. 12:55**) may have been present because of his implied conversion as well. Jude is credited with writing the later epistle which bears his name in the New Testament canon. Church chronicler, Clement of Alexandria in the second century attested to the accepted fact that the epistle to be the work of Jesus' brother, Jude.[46] Therefore to conclude Jude was probably to be counted within the group makes perfect sense as well.

The possible presence of one or more of Jesus' brothers being in attendance at the upper room meeting seems to indicate the significance James' conversion meant to Jesus' siblings. The New Testament never mentions Jesus' appearing to his other brothers or sisters post-resurrection (**Matt. 12:55–56**). Therefore, it is assumed someone other than the resurrected Christ was responsible for the conversion of the siblings, at the very least the conversion of Jude. It seems probable that James would have been the witness who most likely influenced Jude and maybe others of his family to receive Jesus as Savior.

James' influence on Jude seems to be indicated by Jude's opening sentence within his epistle. Jude states he is a "servant of Jesus Christ, and brother of James" (Jude 1). It is telling that Jude seems to bow to the influence of James. While it is recognized that James was heading the church at Jerusalem at the time of this writing and being Jude's brother would have given an air of credibility to the letter, I feel that the tie to James maybe more about family hierarchy than establishing credibility for the letter. It is interesting that no other New Testament author tries to bring authority to his writing outside of the influence of Jesus. Luke nor Mark nor any other writer tries to establish credibility for his writing by linking himself to someone else. Jude alone is the only example we find.

We should consider the implications of Jesus' biological family being in attendance at the upper room meeting described by Luke. These individuals could directly attest to the birth claims regarding Jesus. It is assumed a narrative had already begun within the circle of believers concerning Jesus' origins. Evidence of such a narrative may be visible in the writings of Mark. It is attested by multiple early church fathers that Mark recorded the testimony of the apostle Peter.[47] If this is the case, Mark would have reflected Peter's understanding of Jesus' origins and lineage. In Mark chapter six, Jesus is referred to simply as the son of Mary (**Mark 6:3**). It is interesting that those who had known Jesus so intimately would refer to him simply as the son of Mary and not as the son of Joseph, as it would have been proper to identify an individual with his father's name, living or deceased. But Mark, under the influence of Peter, identifies Jesus as the son of Mary, without the paternal prerogative. This may indeed reflect Peter's own understanding of Jesus being born without the involvement of an earthy father.

There are those who would use this verse to try to authenticate the claims that Mary remained a virgin after Jesus' birth, never mothering other offspring. Therefore, those referred to as Jesus' biological siblings within the gospels were merely step brothers and sisters, likely the children of Joseph by another wife before Mary. However, as discussed earlier the Greek doesn't support this assumption. Again the term used here is *adelphos* meaning "of the same womb."[48] Logically, without the pressure of doctrinal influence, we would understand the siblings named with Jesus as being biologically related from the direct reading of the passage (**Matt. 12:55–56**).

It is also worth noting here the reference used by Matthew and Luke in their respective gospels. Jesus is referred to as "firstborn son" by both writers (**Matt. 1:25; Luke 2.7, 23**). The phrase implying position, not necessarily status. It is likely both men knew Jesus' biological siblings and the testimony of their biological kinship had been well attested. If Mary had indeed remained a perpetual virgin, why would both of these writers not have used the more correct phrase when describing Jesus, to be her "only son?"

More to the point, His siblings attendance at the upper room meeting in Acts says a lot about the family corroborating what was being said of Jesus. Validating the rumors as it were. There are critics who argue Jesus never claimed deity or to be messiah. So, the siblings being in attendance was not a big deal in the mind of the naysayer. This in fact is wrong. In the Gospel of Mark, the writer explains Jesus clearly declared His deity to the Sanhedrin and to the chief priest at his trial recorded in chapter 14:61–62. When asked by Caiaphas if he were indeed the Christ, Jesus responded, "I am: and ye shall see the son of man sitting on the right hand of power, and coming in the clouds of heaven." To this statement Caiaphas tore his clothing believing Jesus to have committed blasphemy. Keep in mind, this is the very charge the Jewish leaders used to convict Jesus and to perpetrate His eventual death sentence (**Matt. 26:65**).

The implications of the siblings' corroboration goes even further, attesting to Jesus' resurrection obviously but also to other claims, such as the virgin birth account. Consider, if there was ever a group of witnesses who could authenticate or deny the stories concerning Jesus this was the group. They had grown up with Him, tried to protect Him, and had witnessed firsthand what He and others said about Him. Never is testimony witnessed from those within this group which offered contradiction to the narrative taking shape around their brother, a carpenter who would be credited with building a bridge from heaven to earth.

James' Orthodoxy

It is also worth discussing the orthodox leanings of James. When considering the positions represented by New Testament writers, James seems to be more in line with traditional views from Jewish faith and practice expressed by the Mosaic Law. The reason for his leanings are very likely attributed to the perspective of the community in which he was raised. I, being raised in the South, am a product of southern beliefs and culture. Community provides a lens through which the individual views the world around him and this would likely be no different for James.

This is not to say other New Testament writers didn't share this same perspective but perhaps James' adherence to Jewish religious practice was a sign of his early commitment to faith. It is interesting that the Bible represents Mary as being "favored" by God (**Luke 1:28**). It may be extrapolated that Mary's early devotion to God is what earned her the honor of becoming the mother of Jesus. It is assumed Mary was quite young when she became pregnant with Jesus.[49] Perhaps, James was simply following the example of his mother. Or perhaps, James might have favored Jewish orthodoxy because it was the very thing his brother was preaching against. Remember that James was as human as the next man. How many siblings throughout the decades ran in opposite directions because of sibling rivalries? Nevertheless, it is through this lens of cultural leanings that we must now gaze to view the next argument in support of the virgin birth narrative.

Often many modern Christians miss that James, and Jesus in this regard, was raised within the rich tradition of Judaism. While the modern pursuit for the "Jewish" or "historical" Jesus has been used to strip Jesus of His divine character and teachings, it must be admitted that Jewish belief and tradition are necessary to truly realize the full depth of who these individuals were and how both men satisfied the tasks to which they were assigned.

Without digging too deep into the theological underpinnings for Jesus' work, it can readily be seen that the mission of Christ's life was to fulfill the demands of the Jewish law as it is laid out in the Old Testament. After all, Jesus explained, "I came not to destroy the law but to fulfill it" (**Matt. 5:17**). By divine design, Jesus' life fulfills prophecy and the demands spelled out in the writings of the Jewish prophets. It is interesting to consider that Jesus' brother James may have provided a similar bridge from the era of law to the era of grace.

When James' epistle is considered, we find much emphasis placed upon the demonstration of belief. James argues that inward faith in Christ results in measured acts of observable expression. He explains dogmatically that faith without works is for all purposes non-existent (**James 2:26**). The idea of works within the life of the Christian is undeniable, for even Jesus tells His disciples, "you shall do greater works than these" (**John 14:12**). So obviously, works have always been the identifiable hallmark of the Christian. After all love is an action—the evidence of the born-again heart—a model which portrays works as resulting from salvation. However, some have accused James of teaching a works based salvation.[50] Such an attitude toward salvation has moved many to reject James' work without giving it the credit it is due and saddle it with being nothing more than regurgitated Judaism, which should be rejected.

It should be understood that James is not advocating a works based salvation for the Christian. He is simply reminding the convert that his life should be filled with the same activities which Jesus displayed (**James 2:16**). James is however, building a wonderful bridge from what many who would come to faith in Christ would understand. Early Christians were predominately Jewish and understood the expectations of Jewish practice. These expectations called for works within the life of the Jew to demonstrate a love for God (**Deut. 24:19**). James' epistle resulted from his experience and from a position he understood and practiced. James faith in Christ didn't change what he knew to be true from Judaism. A love for God results in measurable service. Jesus said He came to fulfill the expectations of the law not to void them (**Matt. 5:17**). Often the Christian sees Judaism as broken. Yes, it is as broken as any religion, however Judaism was the means which was used as a conduit for man to find God before Christ. It is through Judaism God chose to reveal himself to man in the past and through which He sent Christ to redeem mankind. James' understandings of God's revelation and his Jewish foundation are what made him the natural pick to become the de facto leader of the Christian movement and to become the first pastor of the Jerusalem church. He would be a natural guide for those transitioning from Judaism to newfound faith in Christ.

Further, the dedication lauded by James to Judaism as is seen in his epistle offers another example of James' importance in authenticating the tradition of Jesus, particularly the virgin birth narrative. James' orthodoxy toward Judaism would not have allowed him to advocate a lie, even if the lie would elevate his brother to high ethical standing and would allow himself to become the successive leader of the movement his brother started. He knew what the scriptures said about the coming Messiah to Israel and what he had witnessed concerning his brother. Remember, James may not have had a high regard for Jesus before the resurrection event. If what was being said concerning Jesus was nothing but fabricated tales, it is most probable James would have rejected the tales and called out the heresy. This would have been his opportunity to demonstrate how truly unhinged his brother had become and how right he was in trying to intervene into the events that would lead his brother to execution. He had the ability to restore the family honor and to correct all that his brother had done to bring a tarnished opinion upon the family, leaving them viewed as possible instigators of continued insurrection against Judaism and Rome. But James did not do that.

He did not. These three words say so much about what James had come to know as true. The contrast and rivalry between the two brothers seems to vanish in an event which barely garners mention within the New Testament. If Paul had never been forced to prove his credentials to a church in the city of Corinth, readers may have never known the catalyst for James' conversion and of the importance of James' decision to follow the teachings of his brother, Jesus. This conversion was probably what led James' other siblings to belief in Jesus as Messiah. This conversion would become the lynchpin in what would transform a novel movement found in the backwater of Judea into a force that would eventually lead a third of the world's population to belief in Jesus of Nazareth as the Christ.

James' Death

Before ending the discussion of James' importance in validating the birth narrative of Jesus, there is one last point which should be highlighted. This point is James' death. Tradition suggests James was martyred in Jerusalem in the early AD 60s, probably 62 AD. Early church historian, Hegesippus explains James was thrown from the temple pinnacle in Jerusalem by Jewish leaders in hopes of bringing about a swift death because of his vocal belief that Jesus was the Messiah.[51] However, James was later stoned and beaten to finish the job as the impact of the fall did not immediately kill the man. James had lived in Jerusalem for roughly thirty years after Jesus' death and resurrection with little opposition. What changed? The circumstances surrounding his execution are interesting as presented again by Hegesippus.

Hegesippus explains James' execution was the result of Jewish leaders trying to silence rumblings in Jerusalem concerning Jesus as Christ. The Jews came to James demanding him to correct what they believed was misinformation being spread that Jesus was indeed the Christ. James did the opposite and declared Jesus to be the anointed of God.[52] How wonderful it would have been had James' testimony been preserved or recorded line for line. While there is no known written dictation existent of James' words as of this writing, testimony may very well be preserved of what James communicated.

It is my opinion the very testimony James' offered concerning the identity of Jesus and which inevitably led to His death is available. The ideas to which James bore witness are preserved in the pages of Scripture, notably in Luke's gospel account. Consider, there are scholars who believe the critical dating of Luke's gospel said to be around AD 80 is wrong. Some scholars suggest Luke's gospel was written before AD 60 and thus would contain very early traditions and opinions surrounding Jesus. Evidence for dating Luke's work as early includes: no mention of the destruction of Jerusalem by Rome in AD 70, no mention of Christian persecution under Nero, which began around AD 60, and no mention of the deaths of either Peter, James, or Paul in the early AD 60s.[53] If this evidence is correct, Luke's work would reflect ideas and positions embraced by the church's earliest leadership.

Traditions contained in Luke's work would have been known by James as he headed up the church at Jerusalem prior to his death around AD 62. It is likely that the very record Luke used to write his gospel may have been made up of James' memories provided to Paul during Paul's visit to Jerusalem three years after his conversion. Remember, Luke is thought to have been Paul's traveling companion on occasion and had access to the information collected by Paul. If further extrapolation is utilized, then it is probable that the testimony James gave to Paul concerning Jesus continued unchanged and unredacted and was thus communicated to those who would execute James for this same testimony.

As stated earlier within this chapter, James was the perfect person to provide detail concerning the early life of the Savior. He would have been present for a great deal of Jesus' life. And for those years or events which he wasn't present, testimony he had grown up hearing from his mother and father would have provided detail. Yes, this testimony to which I refer would have included the miraculous conception event and the details surrounding the nativity story.

Attention will now be turned to the collection of many of the details surrounding Jesus' life. The collector being none other than Luke. Luke provides the greatest historical account of the beginnings of the Christian saga.

While author bias is always present in any work of human origin, Luke does an exceptional job of recording the events detailing the story of Jesus and the work which He started.

6

That You May Know with Certainty

———⊰⊱———

Forasmuch as many have taken in hand to set forth in order a declaration of those things which are most surely believed among us.
(Luke 1:1)

Let us consider Luke's work. Luke seems to be the perfect candidate to record the story of the advancement of the church and its birth related to the story of Jesus. Luke stands on the periphery of many of the events he describes providing his reader firsthand knowledge of what is happening and the motives behind the decisions being made. This is not to say Luke was a silent spectator, but rather he had a wonderful vantage point from which to observe and report details few others could.

There is some speculation as to what role Luke may have played, if any, within the activities of the budding church before his work with Paul.[54] It has been suggested he may have been part of the larger number of disciples who followed Jesus' ministry but for this present discussion, Luke's activities as identified within the pages of the Bible will be the only information considered. He can be seen as a fellow laborer of the gospel, a loyal encourager and personal caregiver within the Bible. But with all the hats he may have worn, Luke's work as faithful transcriptionist might be described as his most worthwhile and greatest contribution to the church. Luke's vocation is listed by Paul as being a doctor (**Col. 4:14**). His background in the sciences made him pay special attention to details and, as a doctor, he was interested in what could be measured and quantified to produce the positive. As a historian, his disciplined approach to the world around him would produce the most comprehensive treatment of the story of the church depicted (**Luke 1:3**).

Consider, Luke did not write to become forever memorialized as a contributor to a new collection of holy books. Luke was simply writing to inform one individual named Theophilus concerning the story of the church, from the days of Jesus its founder, to its modern manifestation within his day (**Luke 1:1–4; Acts 11**). The true identity of Theophilus remains a mystery but the need he represents can be glimpsed in the faces of all those who have ever set out to read Luke's work. Luke's chief motivation was to inform and provide an orderly account of the historical record. He explains there were sources floating around which provided details about various aspects of Jesus' story and the church tradition. Essentially, Luke hoped to provide a clearer, comprehensive record so his reader, who may have been new to the faith at the time of the writing, could easily understand and comprehend.[55]

There are points which jump off the page of Luke's prologue which should pique the interest of anyone reading this narrative which Luke addresses to Theophilus. First, the statement "those things which are most surely believed among us" seems to allude to a consensus being reached within a group. Who is the group to which Luke is referring? I believe the identity of the group rests with the apostle Paul. Only speculation to the size can be offered but participants may be obtained by reading the works of Luke's friend and mentor. Paul's list of group members likely includes names such as John Mark, Luke, Demas, Aristarchus, Timothy, Titus, Barnabas, Silas, and others (**Rom. 16:21–23; 1 Cor. 16, 17–20; Phil. 4:21; Col. 4:10–17**). Why is identifying members of this group important? Because, each of these men would be influenced by Paul and the information he had collected. These men would sit at the feet of this prolific apostle, learning theological application and historical truth few had ever considered. Also, each of these men would become leaders of ministries of the their own eventually, passing along the same ideas and information explored and debated among this group. Considering this company as students is very reminiscent of the many conversations and discussions I recall from my own days in seminary.

I remember ideas and theories explored amongst my fellow academics offered from a mutual desire to simply understand the why and how God did what He did to produce the opportunity of redemption. We know from our own experience that any individual is simply a product of the ideas and experiences he encounters whether good or bad in this life. In my case, the good I experienced at seminary would produce the heart of a pastor. To this present discussion, the good Paul poured into his companions would produce individuals who would help shape the infant church into the global powerhouse it would become (**Luke 1:1–4**).

In the opening lines of his gospel, Luke is not only saying what he has prepared for Theophilus is the product of his personal opinion, but is the consensus of the group. A consensus the group had speculated over, argued about, and ultimately had reached, which is considered the most logical treatise based upon the facts at hand (**1 Cor. 15:3–8**). This group's concluding consensus would lend needed weight to Luke's treatment of the information he records for Theophilus, particularly to subjects like the controversial virgin birth narrative.

Secondly, notice Luke's use of the phrase "as they delivered them to us" (**Luke 1:2**) as being very similar to the phrase Paul uses when he addresses the Corinthian church with the gospel in chapter 15 of his first letter (**1 Cor. 15:3**). Who exactly was responsible for delivering the facts Luke supplies to Theophilus? It is my opinion that Luke is probably referring to the information first given to Paul. As referenced earlier, this information was probably provided by the Apostles Peter and James at Paul's first meeting with the men three years after his conversion (**Gal. 1:18–20**). Paul describes this meeting in his letter to the Galatian church. The men were passing along what they had seen, heard, and witnessed. Luke may be identifying these same sources in a roundabout way when he states "which from the beginning were eyewitnesses, and ministers of the word" (**Luke 1:2; Matt. 4:18–20; Mark 6:3**). There would have been no better candidates than Peter and James to relay important information such as the virgin birth occurrence.

Further, Peter and James had both been ministering sometime before Paul would begin his ministry to the church. As a matter of fact, Paul is actually painted as a product of the work of these two men, and others as well. In totality, the two were with Jesus from His youth until His ascension into heaven (**Luke 1:2; Matt. 13:55; Acts1:1–9**). They would have been the authorities on all things Jesus. It is therefore likely both would have provided their opinions and perspectives on the virginity story of Mary and of the miraculous conception event.

It is also worth exploring here an idea I once heard addressed many years ago by Liberty University Professor,

Dr. Gary Habermas. Dr. Habermas was a visiting professor at Temple Baptist Seminary (Now Piedmont Divinity School) where I attended. Habermas spoke on the idea that early creeds were often recorded within the pages of Scripture.[56] These creeds would reflect the basic beliefs held by early Christians in an easy to remember format which could be committed to memory and passed along to new converts. Luke's use of the phrase used by Paul "as they delivered them to us" could be an indication that what Luke may have been using as part of his source material could have been a creed familiar to the Christian community. This creed could have contained information regarding Jesus' origin story, along with other details. This would show commonality of belief within the early Christian community.

So why are these points important in regards to the present discussion? These points bear witness to the fact Luke wasn't simply concocting a fanciful tale out of thin air about Jesus' birth story. Luke was conveying what was being discussed and reported by the larger community of Christians. Luke is the only gospel writer to report the miraculous conception story of Jesus. Some may find this odd, but when you consider Luke's perspective this makes perfect sense. Most writers would focus attention on the miraculous works Jesus performs, along with His teachings. With the writing of the other gospels accounts, this is exactly what is portrayed as these were witnessed by the apostles who walked with Jesus and who were responsible for the other gospel accounts. How overwhelming it must have been to see such power demonstrated by Jesus! Matthew and John report exactly from this perspective of awe and wonder. Mark is generally understood to be reporting for Peter and likewise, Mark chronicles Peter's veneration. However, Luke is writing from the perceptive of the apostle Paul.

Paul was a pharisee by training. While Jesus' miracles were amazing to behold, the Pharisees knew that miracles were made possible only by the anointing of God (**1 Kings 18:38**). Miracles were well documented within the sacred writings. In the mind of the Pharisees, the stamp of God upon the true Messiah would have been his pedigree even more so than the signs and wonders Jesus' performs (**Matt. 2:4–6**). Pharisees knew what to look for even in the origin of the Messiah. This anointed man would assume the throne of King David and lead the nation to autonomy from foreign rule (**2 Sam. 7:12–16**). Jewish tradition taught Messiah would be born from an *alma* or virgin, as noted earlier in this work, from the royal seed of David (**Isa. 7:14; Ps. 132:11**). This virgin would give birth to the anointed. This is the one single element of Messiah's origin which would set him apart from other heirs born within the lineage of David and make him the rightful successor to sit upon the throne of Israel.

Paul was able to connect the dots within Jesus' story that others may not have seen or even knew existed. Paul would become the great apologist demonstrating how

Jesus fulfilled what was expected of Messiah (**Titus 2:13**). Paul would provide answers to pressing questions and/or objections made by the Jewish community (**Acts 18:28**). After collecting information concerning Jesus, Paul knew the significance of what he had uncovered in Jesus' backstory. Anyone could claim to be Messiah but there could only be one who had the true pedigree of Messiah. Paul recognized Jesus fulfilled of all the Messianic requirements from front to back and was bent on telling the world.

It is important to remember that the narrative being reported by Luke was never rebutted by his contemporaries within the church, Paul included. Some would argue Paul had been executed long before Luke's gospel was completed. Even if Paul did not personally get to witness the completion of Luke's work, this does not change the point being made. There were many other men who travelled and sat under the teachings of Paul as discussed. Paul's teachings would have continued to outlive him in the minds of those who were groomed under him. Yet, none challenged Luke's report nor his presentation that Christ was virgin born. Timothy nor Titus nor any of the others would refute Luke's manuscript. They could have corrected the record if warranted. They could attest to what Paul had taught in the churches he planted and to the group of young ministers he trained for leadership. They could attest to what Paul had instructed them while they were under his direction. They could attest to the details he provided concerning Jesus and His story. But again, no one challenged Luke's volume.

Earlier, it was explained there were those who could provide firsthand detail regarding things like growing up and ministering with Jesus. Peter and James were the witnesses to which I turned to demonstrate this point. However, these were not the only two eyewitness accounts to which a person could turn to provide details for Jesus' historical events. Paul is quoted as explaining there were hundreds still living who could verify the gospel message he carried to the Corinthians (**1 Cor. 15:6**). Paul's point was correct. There were mere years that had transpired between the events he details and the recording of the events, which meant there were individuals still living who could provide eyewitness testimony. Harold Willmington writes, "[Paul] probably wrote 1 Corinthians near the end of his time in Ephesus, AD 56."[57] If someone had hoped to dispel the Jesus' story, the host of witnesses which could attest to the reality of who Jesus was and to details concerning his life could easily have been called on to set the record straight.

This means there was hard, historical support which could verify the story of Jesus and other events surrounding the early church offered by multiple witnesses. Consider other religious persuasions, normally there is only the testimony of one who becomes the sole oracle who provides witness to a message being preached. For example, Muhammad transcribing the message of Allah,

Joseph Smith producing the tablets supposedly provided him by the angel Moroni, and Ellen G. White writing her commentaries to the Seventh-day Adventists, are all examples of one lonely voice advocating for the divine origin of their individual message. However, this is not the case with the story of Jesus or of the church. One voice is never relied solely upon. Jesus explained there should be multiple witnesses called upon to give testimony concerning anything which is disputed and multiple witnesses are provided attesting to the events described in the gospel (**Matt. 18:16**). Luke is simply one of the many whose work became one of the most trusted.

Early Date for Luke's Gospel

The argument for the later date of Luke's gospel is built on the assumption that Luke used the Gospel of Mark as source material. Mark is thought to have been written after AD 70 because Mark references the destruction of the temple at Jerusalem (**Mark 13:1–37**). Textual critics largely reject the miracles of Jesus and likewise, dismiss Jesus' prophecies as well (**Matt. 24**). They reason Jesus' prophetic utterances were only attributed to Him after the event had occurred. The prophecies recorded by the gospel authors, so say the critics, are there to simply provide a facade of omniscience to the man whose followers claimed to be God on earth.

In the case of Mark's reference to the destruction of Herod's Temple by the Romans (**Mark 13**), history dates the event to AD 70 and thus, the critics argue Mark's reference of the event in his work happened sometime after it occurred.[58] The dating of Mark's gospel account is reasoned to be around AD 70 and Luke's gospel is therefore dated later still, because the critic assumes Luke used Mark as source material for his work. However, if Jesus was in fact who He said He was, God in the flesh, He could easily have predicted the destruction of the temple before it occurred (**Mark 14:61–62**).

Interestingly, there may be evidence suggesting that Luke's work is older than the critics suggest. Consider, Paul may have quoted from Luke. In his letter to Timothy, Paul writes, "a laborer deserves his wages" (**1 Tim. 5:18**). This reference seems to come directly from the Gospel of Luke (**Luke 10:17**). If this is indeed the case, the possibility of an earlier date for Luke's gospel must be contemplated. Paul is executed in the early AD 60s.[59] So, this could mean Luke wrote his gospel earlier than the critical date of sometime later than AD 70 if Paul is to have quoted from it.

With all likelihood, it should be accepted that all of the gospel accounts are considerably older than critical scholarship allows. Most reasonable students understand Christ's abilities as God would allow Him to do many things the performance of which are deemed impossible by the mortal. His ability to rightly predict future events actually seems quite easy compared to raising the dead. Yet, He is described as being able to do both. The accounts which record Jesus' prophecies are likely legitimate transcriptions and should be received as such with dates of completion far closer to conservative opinions.[60]

While he could have, Luke would not have had to use Mark as source material. I believe Luke is probably relying more heavily on Paul's notes more than any other source. So, why do the synoptic gospels match so closely in detail? It is quite simple really. Mark and Paul were both relying on the same testimony of Peter. It must be remembered Paul went to gain the back story of Jesus from Peter and James (**Gal.1:18–20**). Peter relayed to Paul his memories of his time spent with Jesus. Paul was a good student and wrote down what Peter told him likely providing Luke the source material he would one day use to write his gospel. Peter was also the source for Mark's gospel, according to early church fathers.[61] It is likely that Luke and Mark were ultimately using the same source, Peter. How does Matthew figure into the equation? He lived the events with Peter as the original twelve apostles traveled ministering with Jesus over the span of about three years. I can't but help thinking it amusing to consider Peter as the true *Q* source for at least two of the gospel accounts. What is the *Q* source? The *Q* source is suggested to be a fabled, ancient volume which is said to have recorded all the common material which

Matthew, Mark, and Luke used to write the canonical gospel accounts.[62]

Some reject an early date for the writing of the gospels because the theology of Christianity appears too developed in the works. However if Jesus is who He said He was, He would have been teaching refined theology with no help needed from later contributors to mature or refine his message. There is evidence of His extraordinary teaching ability and His presentation of advanced theology even at an early age attested to by Luke (**Luke 2:39–52**). The arrogance of scholars implying Jesus would not have had the ability to present a mature rendering of theology is mind-numbing. He was the originator of Christian theology. Just call to mind the event recorded by Luke of Jesus being found in the temple teaching the religious scholars of His day. These scholars are presented as being astounded. The irony is noticeable to the objective student of Christianity. Today's scholars need to come down from their self-aggrandizing high horses and humble themselves before the same Christ who, at age twelve, confounded the wisest of His day.

It also seems ironic that many within the church today and many within the circles of modern scholarship are reacting to Jesus with much the same arrogance which was used to charge Christ with blasphemy at His trial before the Jewish authorities (**Matt. 26:65**). Jesus came teaching the way to God (**John 14:6**). He came down from heaven to teach men the way to God because men couldn't find it on their own (**John 3:11–13**). The fact He came from heaven attests to His authority. But the scholars of His day didn't like what He was saying because it undermined their own opinions and suppositions. The reason it was so important to record what Jesus was teaching is because it was unlike anything that had ever been heard or taught. It is even recorded in Scripture that those who heard Him teach were astonished (**Mark 1:22**). Jesus' teachings and actions were so great that John the apostle was prompted to conclude that there were not enough volumes in the world to contain them (**John 21:25**). It seems irrefutable therefore that a refined theology was taught by Jesus from the very beginning of His ministry. It was not something which required theologians over long years to ponder and determine. Jesus was and continues to be the great revelator, the truth. Mark and the other gospel writers simply captured what Jesus was teaching. These men were not refining Jesus' words to fashion a theology, they were simply transcriptionists recording the message which Jesus preached within their lifetimes often in their presence.

Now that adequate consideration has been given to Luke's investigation, attention should be placed upon the individual where Paul and/or Luke could have retrieved tremendous first-person testimony for their work on the virgin birth, Mary, the mother of Jesus. It is often forgotten that Mary would have most likely been the original source for the information many of the earliest Christians had on Jesus' origin. She would have been alive and available to provide details for the birth narrative which no one else could.

7

Mary Knew

———⚭———

*But Mary kept all these things,
and pondered them in her heart.*
(Luke 2:19)

After spending much time deliberating the source materials of this work, it is my position that Jesus' mother's testimony, Mary's, is likely the greatest voice presented advocating for virgin birth. Multiple reasons have lead me to this conclusion which will be shared within this chapter. The eyewitness testimony of Mary will be considered first.

As with other assertions made within this book, this point will likely be challenged by some who read it. However, it seems obvious to me that Mary's first-person testimony is recorded within the pages of Scripture, particularly by Luke. Luke tells the reader his intent is to represent the facts concerning Jesus as accurately as possible

(**Luke 2:1–4**). If this indeed is the case, Luke probably consulted with as many sources and eyewitnesses as he could. While Paul's investigation into the roots of the church contributed greatly to Luke's work, Luke likely followed up with Paul's sources and had his own conversations with individuals as he worked to put words to paper (**Luke 2:2**). One such conversation was likely held with Mary, the mother of Jesus.

Consider, Luke's narrative concerning Mary contains many personal details describing her words, feelings, and actions that are not recorded by other writers. The few details presented by other writers are generic and seem to be third-person retellings of what others told of events. This is not the case with Luke. Luke even records private conversations and personal events which only Mary could accurately recount, key among them her conversation with the angel Gabriel (**Luke 1:28**). More to the point, his words capture Mary's state of mind, feelings, and reflections regarding her personal response within the birth story record (**Luke 1:29**). Such detail could only be collected by speaking to the individual who had lived the event (**Luke 2:19**).

It was shortly after rereading the nativity, just before beginning this work, that it dawned on me that Luke could have spoken to Mary firsthand, as could have Paul, Peter, and John, for Mary would have been available to these Christian journalists. Remember, as stated earlier, Mary was with the apostles in the upper room in the opening chapter of Acts (**Acts 1:13–14**). Jesus had left her in the care of John the apostle prior to His death on Calvary (**John 19:26**). And according to history, she continued to live under the care of John until her death shortly after 40 AD.[63]

It is interesting how God works. He likes to work against the normal flow of human experience at times, as is the case of Mary as witness for the virgin birth story. Being a woman, Mary's testimony at this moment in history would not have been admissible in Jewish legal proceedings.[64] Therefore, her witness to this monumental event would have been suspect in the mind of many of her day. However, God uses her as the greatest voice to convey the message of this miraculous event. Luke would not have simply pulled such a claim from thin air to include as proof of Jesus' origins. He was a smart individual who knew that such a wild claim would likely cause many readers to question and even reject his gospel account, particularly Theophilus (**Luke 1:3**). However, the use of Mary's testimony in the origin story makes it that much more believable because if Luke was making the story up, he would have used a man for affirmation of the event, perhaps Joseph if he were available. Why? Because at the time a man's voice would have been admissible in legal proceedings, but the voice of a Jewish woman telling the story would have been unthinkable to include as witness testimony even in storytelling.

Concerning the miraculous conception claim, Luke was a doctor by trade, a man of science (**Col. 4:14**). He knew how babies were made. It seems plausible he may have even questioned such a claim when he first heard about Mary's miraculous conception. Obviously, someone was telling the story for it to become a part of Luke's literary work. Luke had witnessed firsthand the power of Christ during his travels with Paul (**Acts 16:6–10; 20:4–21;19**). He knew there was indeed something remarkably different about this Jesus. He knew Jesus was no ordinary man (**Acts 20:7**). Luke was determined to tell Jesus' story because of the power he witnessed that was associated with Jesus' name (**Acts 20:19**). He chose to include the miraculous conception event in his telling because he likely heard the story from the lips of those he trusted, but of more significance he may well have heard that story from Mary herself, and because of what he had witnessed personally concerning Jesus and the work which continued to follow Him even these many years after His crucifixion (**Acts 20:10–12**).

Consider the practical context, the place of compromise in which Mary would have placed herself if her words of miraculous conception were simply a tale. Remember, a person who was thought to have committed fornication was to have been stoned (**Deut. 22:23**). However, Mary was chosen to become the mother of Jesus because of her virtue (**Luke 1:28, 38**). A part of that virtue was no doubt her modesty, which can also be described as her commitment to doing what was right. It seems highly unlikely Mary would have chosen to have committed fornication because she knew the weighty penalty which would follow should she be caught. People in America have forgotten how effective applied penalties can be for deterring unwanted behavior. But Mary being the observant Jewish girl she was, would have probably not needed the deterrent of punishment. She was young and more likely than not, would have still felt an obligation to uphold the values and virtue taught her by her parents.

It should be understood however even if Mary's virtue is accepted, Mary's pregnancy would have been seen as scandalous (**Matt. 1:19**). One can only imagine the tales which were told, especially as she became unable to conceal the pregnancy. Churches have throughout the years whitewashed the story, making the events surrounding the nativity a solemn and virtuous occasion. While it was those things spiritually speaking, it would have probably looked much more like one of the soap operas women once enjoyed on afternoon television in years past. I believe ridicule can be witnessed even within the pages of Scripture as Mark records an event where Jesus returned home to Nazareth preaching and teaching. Mark records the astonishment of the crowd on one particular Sabbath when the people asked, "Isn't this the carpenter? Isn't this Mary's son?" (**Mark 6.1–3**). While some readers might believe the remark was simply the witnesses at the event dismissing Jesus as just a guy from the neighborhood, they all knew too well. It is my opinion the crowd was dismissing Jesus as the illegitimate son of Mary. They were implying the question, what business has he preaching to us. Notice there is no mention of his earthly father, Joseph. Sons were typically known by the lineage of the father (**Mark 10:35**). In Hebrew men were usually called "bara" or "son of," thusly Jesus would have been known as Jesus son of Joseph (**Luke 3:23**). But here, Mark records this is not the case. Remember many of these people would have known Mary as a young lady and would have remembered the scandal surrounding her pregnancy with Jesus. Yet, Mary maintained her story. She never wavered in the retelling. This is commendable as she could have jeopardized her well-being and no doubt, compromised her name. But she stayed true to the retelling of the events that led up to the birth of her firstborn son (**Luke 1:26–56**).

You may be unaware of the scandalous account of Jesus' origin which was cited and rebuffed by the Christian writer Origen in the second century within his work, *Contra Celsum* or "Against Celsus." Celsus was a second century Greek writer and philosopher who had a particular distain for Christianity. Celsus imagined that Jesus' mother Mary had an affair with a Roman soldier named Pantera.[65] Celsus goes as far as to claim Mary was publicly convicted of adultery with the soldier. Of course, there is no historical proof of such a relationship nor is there evidence of such a conviction. If such events had occurred, Luke obviously would not have presented Mary as a virgin at the time of Jesus' birth. In fact, he probably would not have included the birth story in his work at all. It would have been too easy for someone to have pushed back against the ruse Luke was trying to sell in his gospel account. Celsus' story was offered with no supporting evidence whatsoever. It seems laughable that someone could offer such an outrageous accusation decades after the event of Jesus' life. But this example does show us that the ingredients for scandal did surround the events of Jesus' birth and there were individuals, just as today, who were ready to undermine the gospel narrative with a salacious backstory.

In the foregoing review, we've witnessed an unwavering commitment to the virgin birth account as told by Mary and recorded by Luke. Often claims are made regarding a person or an event, but over time such accusations either prove true or the legs on which these allegations stand deteriorate. While scholars and/or dissidents have feverishly worked to undermine the story of Jesus' miraculous conception, they have been unable to disapprove Luke's record. If anyone knew Jesus was virgin born, Mary did.

Silence at the Cross

Probably the most impactful testimony regarding the virgin birth account is Mary's silence at the cross.

When we read the crucifixion accounts within the gospels, Mary is portrayed as being heartbroken but silent as she watches Jesus endure the rigors of crucifixion (**John 19:25–27**).[66] This is remarkable. Most parents will defend their children to the very end. Many parents would even die in the place of their children. Parents normally plead the innocence of their child regardless whether the child was caught red-handed violating the law. I have known several mothers and grandmothers over the course of my ministry who have defended a child even when it was plain to see the child was involved in mischief to say the least. Mary's silence as Jesus is executed is remarkable. So why did she stay silent?

The fact is, there was really nothing Mary could say. Jesus was guilty of the infraction He was eventually crucified for committing. He was crucified because He was God (**John 10:30-33**). He admitted His identity to His accusers. There are those who say Jesus never claimed to be God but that statement is made from ignorance of the gospel account. Jesus made the observation in Matthew 22, "ye do err, not knowing the scriptures, nor the power of God" (**Matt. 22:29**). The statement is certainly true of those who deny that Jesus made the claim to be the Deity. Mark 14 is very clear that Jesus did indeed make known His identify. Mark writes, "Again the high priest asked him, and said unto him, Art thou the Christ, the Son of the Blessed? And Jesus said, I am" (**Mark 14:61–62**). The priests assumed Jesus blasphemed God by making the statement because Jesus was making himself equal to God. However, His statement was true because He was God and for that, Jesus was crucified.

Mary knew Jesus' claim was true. There was nothing she could say which could rebut His testimony concerning His identity. She knew Jesus was telling the truth about who he was. She remembered the angel's visit before she had miraculously conceived her son in her womb (**Luke 1:26–38**). She remembered the relief of finding Jesus teaching in the temple at age twelve after losing Him for days (**Luke 2:41–52**). She remembered watching the miracle He performed at the wedding in Cana when He turned the water to wine (**John 2:1–12**). She knew who Jesus was and there was no denying all she had witnessed. Jesus' wisdom and abilities could only be explained as supernatural. There was no mistaking the fact that Jesus was God in the flesh and Mary knew it. However, the Jewish leadership delivered Him to be crucified because they didn't believe His claims and were envious of His ministry (**Matt. 27:18**). They didn't want anyone rocking the status-quo.

In one of his stand-up routines, Christian comedian Mark Lowry made the observation that if anyone knew Jesus was virgin born, Mary did. Lowry made the observation that if Jesus wasn't who He said He was, Mary surely would have intervened with the Jewish authorities by pleading, "He [Jesus] is crazy but don't kill him." Indeed Lowry is right. Any mother worth her title would have intervened for her child's life and Mary was no different. But she knew what Jesus said was true and there was nothing she could do but weep over the tragedy which was being perpetrated upon her son. Lowry is famous for writing the lyrics of the popular Christmas musical classic, "Mary, Did You Know?"[67] To which the author responds affirmatively, yes. Mary knew and that is what silenced her has she stood helpless to save her son from the rigors of the cross.

Conclusion

Mary is indeed the greatest single voice supporting the miraculous conception story. She knew her son was something remarkable and the only explanation she or anyone else could offer was that Jesus was in fact the Son of God. While Mary may have been the first to truly know and understand Jesus' origins, many others would come to know that His miraculous birth was true. Jesus healed multitudes of people, forever changing lives. He preached about the kingdom of God and revealed the path people could walk to become part of this kingdom (**Matt. 7:14**). Even today, Jesus continues to touch people through the opportunity of salvation He alone offers (**John 3:16–21**). Lives are no longer lived in desperation or despair. Jesus continues His work of bringing salvation to the lost today just as He did two thousand years ago.

This work will now consider the abundant testimony of Jesus' words and works and how they continue to testify to His miraculous origins. Keep in mind that no one has ever had such things attributed to them as did Jesus. Even secular first-century Jewish historian Flavius Josephus alludes to the extraordinary deeds of Jesus in his work *Jewish Antiquities* where he wrote, "About this time there lived a wise man, if indeed one ought to call him a man. For he was one who performed surprising deeds and was a teacher of such people as accept the truth gladly."[68] You should judge for yourself if Jesus was indeed who He claimed to be by considering the testimony He offered about himself.

8

Jesus' Words and Works

---

*He answered and said, Whether he be a sinner or no,
I know not: one thing I know, that,
whereas I was blind, now I see.*
(John 9:25)

The above verse is my very favorite. Wow. What a testimony this blind man delivers. There is an old saying, "the proof of the pudding is in the eating." How fitting is this line of reasoning for this chapter? What Jesus was able to deliver through His words and works was beyond earthly explanation except He be sent by God, which is what the story of the blind man is really all about (**John 9:68**).

Continue to read the exchange between the once blind man and the Pharisees as recorded in John 9:

We know that God spake unto Moses: as for this fellow, we know not from whence he is.

The man answered and said unto them, Why herein is a marvelous thing, that ye know not from whence he is, and yet he hath opened mine eyes.

Now we know that God heareth not sinners: but if any man be a worshipper of God, and doeth his will, him he heareth.

Since the world began was it not heard that any man opened the eyes of one that was born blind.

If this man were not of God, he could do nothing. (**John 9:29–33**)

This once blind man chose to recognize Jesus as God based upon the impact of Jesus' work on his life (**John 9:38**). Note the blind man's use of the word *Lord* in his exchange with Jesus, "And he said, Lord, I believe. And he worshipped him." The Greek translates the word *Lord* to *kuros*, which can mean "supremacy."[69] The choice of words used by the blind man seems to present Jesus as being superior when contrasted to the leaders who berated the man for his improved condition. But more to the point, the meaning supports the blind man's acknowledgement of Jesus as God based upon the work he received from Jesus. More on this in a moment.

This seems a very logical approach to most things in life. If something or someone is able to produce positive results, this means there is reason to embrace the producer. Thus, the results of Jesus' ministry should be proof positive to substantiate His claims of being God (**John 10:30**) as no man has ever been able to reproduce the results Jesus did. "But if I do, though ye believe not me, believe the works: that ye may know, and believe, that the Father *is* in me, and I in him" (**John 10:38**). Plainly, Jesus states that His works should tell the story, without doubt, of His identity. However many people of His day deliberately chose not to acknowledge what the signs were clearly telling them (**John 10:39**).

For the blind man, Jesus' works led him to acknowledge Jesus as God (**John 9:38**). The Bible details he "worshipped" Jesus. The Greek can mean that the blind man "prostrated" himself before Jesus in an act of "profound reverence."[70] Interestingly, this very same act of "worship" is attributed to the wise men which came from the east who sought out Jesus sometime after his birth (**Matt. 2:11**). So it seems that while some people ignored the signs pointing to Jesus' Deity, others were able to read the same signs with clear detail.

Ironically, as the verses cited earlier tell the reader, Moses was recognized as an instrument of God's hand by many of the same people who rejected Jesus (**John**

9:38). Moses' selection as God's man was evident to those Jews who were distancing themselves from Jesus because Moses' remarkable assignment had been detailed in the holy writings (**Exod. 34:30**). In fact, Moses encountered dissidents just as Jesus, even as God's validation of Moses was clearly visible to the nation in the pillar which always went before them on their journey out of Egypt (**Num. 11–17**). Just as God provided a sign through the pillar to their ancestors, God was providing signs through Jesus' miracles validating His ministry, identity, and by extension, his miraculous conception. If Jesus wasn't who he said he was, God simply could have barred Him from performing the miracles which provided support for His claims. But the generation into which Jesus came had become so distant from God they refused to recognize God and His activities, even when He showed up in their very midst (**Matt. 16:4**). Jesus never tried to conceal His identity, He plainly proclaimed His divinity (**John 10:30, 31; Mark 14:61, 62**) and argued His miraculous works should validate His identity. Observe Jesus' statement, "Jesus answered them, Many good works have I shewed you from my Father; for which of those works do ye stone me?" (**John 10:32**).

Further, we should consider the blind man's rationale. He observes the evidence and the evidence leads him to a conclusion, which is logical. No man has ever been able to do the things Jesus did says the man, therefore the explanation must mean Jesus is not a mere man

(**John 9:33**). There must be something supernatural about Jesus in order to explain His remarkable abilities. This is the conclusion the man makes. Note the man's response, "Lord, I believe. And he worshipped him" (**John 9:38**). Many read the blind man's response to Jesus and see no motivation in his statement that would lead us to believe the blind man thought Jesus was God. But obviously, this opinion is wrong.

Consider further, the blind man follows up his statement with the act of worshipping Jesus as John records. If the blind man wasn't convinced that Jesus was God, he would not have revered Jesus through the act of worship. Also, there is a deeper acknowledgment being made by the man in his statement. The title he uses to acknowledge Jesus is more than simply a designation thrown around loosely, as some would postulate. The word *Lord*, or *kuros* in Greek has an interesting usage as employed in the Greek Septuagint translation of the Old Testament (**Jer. 3:23**). In the majority of times *Lord* or *kuros* is used by the Septuagint translators, the word is being used to designate the Hebrew name Yahweh, which is the personal name of the God of Israel (**Gen. 2:4, Deut. 8:18**).[71] While this is certainly an interesting parallel, many readers still miss the weight with which the blind man identifies Jesus. This blind man being from a good Jewish home would have been very familiar with the Tanakh or Old Testament scriptures (**John 9:22**). However, many students of the Bible still miss the fact that the majority of households in first century Judah would have been more familiar with the Greek Septuagint Old Testament than the Hebrew version of the same work.[72] The blind man's use of the term *Lord* or *kuros* to acknowledge Jesus was the blind man's way of testifying to Jesus' deity as Yahweh. The man knew the term was used to designate the personal God of Israel in the scriptures and he was using the same term to designate Jesus as his personal God of Israel. This acknowledgment by the man and probably others is what ultimately set the Jewish authorities against Jesus, for not only was Jesus claiming to be associated with Yahweh, but Jesus was being identified as Yahweh.

It is interesting to consider that the Jewish authorities may have left Jesus be, if He was simply claiming to be God. It is easy to dismiss the rantings of someone who could be called mentally unhinged. What ultimately became the problem was that the population surrounding Jesus began to acknowledge Him as God (**John 4:42**). The consensus was being fueled by the many miracles they watched Jesus' work (**Matt. 14:3**). As long as no one bought His silly claims of being God incarnate, He was harmless, the authorities must have thought. They would have seen Jesus as someone to be pitied rather than someone to be feared. He would have simply been seen as someone missing a few rocks, being shy of a load. However, Jesus' works seemed to authenticate His origin claims and the crowds began to take notice of the evidence (**John 10:30–33**).

John the Baptist confirms the blind man's conclusion in John 3 "He that cometh from above is above all: he that is of the earth is earthly, and speaketh of the earth: he that cometh from heaven is above all" (**John 3:31**). When presented with tangible evidence, the conclusion must logically consider the observed facts. This is what logical reasoning, or the scientific method, teaches. However, many who advocate for logical reasoning reject Jesus as nothing more than a liar or lunatic. Jesus' work continues to be plainly visible to all who care to notice, even today. The sick are healed today as they were in the pages of Scripture. Chains of bondage are broken in people's lives today as they were in Jesus' time on earth. And, countless numbers turn to Jesus every day for the promise of salvation as they did when He walked physically among men. All of this was accomplished then and continues to be accomplished today by the continued work of Jesus. Yet, Jesus is mocked and maligned for only producing good in the lives of those who trust Him. Why does this continue?

The answer is witnessed as the blind man's story unfolds. Many today continue to make the same mistakes that the Pharisees of Jesus' day were guilty of making. They deliberately choose not to believe the evidence which was clearly in front of them (**John 9:18–20**). There was no denying Jesus was different than other preachers and prophets who walked the dusty roads of Judea during the first century (**John 7:46**). He was not simply offering promises of condemnation or blessing upon the nation.

He was actually healing the sick, raising the dead, and offering access to the kingdom of God. Yet, the religious leaders who were supposed to know God, chose to dismiss the opportunities Jesus offered (**John 14:7**). These individuals consciously closed their eyes to the person and work of Jesus and called for Him to be executed because He threatened the status quo (**Matt. 27:5**). They even threaten blackmail toward the Roman Procurator if the job wasn't done to suit them (**John 19:15**).

Note the exchange which continues between the Pharisees and Jesus in the conclusion of John 9, "Are we blind also? (the Pharisees ask), Jesus said unto (the Pharisees), If ye were blind, ye should have no sin: but now ye say, We see; therefore your sin remaineth (vv. 40, 41). Jesus' identity was on full display before these religious leaders but instead of embracing Jesus, they chose to crucify Him. Harold Willmington of Liberty University writes regarding this exchange, "(Jesus) stated the paradox that permeates the story: Those claiming the most spiritual sight are often the most spiritually blind."[73] Sadly, this is the same condition affecting many today.

There are individuals I have come across during my years of ministry who genuinely have asked whether there is proof that supports the claim of Jesus being God incarnate. Some have asked, "How can I know for certain that Jesus was and is God?" Besides Jesus' own declaration in Mark 14:62, we need only consider the attributes of God and compare these with what is observed in Jesus' testimony. While there are many attributes which could be considered, for the sake of space, only three will be explored here as unique to God:

God is omnipresent (He is everywhere.),
God is omnipotent (He is all-powerful.), and
God is omniscient (He is all-knowing.).

Are these attributes of divinity witnessed in what is known of Jesus from the New Testament? Yes!

Consider Jesus' statement in Matthew 18 for evidence of His omnipresence. Jesus states, "For where two or three are gathered together in My name, I am there in their midst" (**Matt. 18:20**). All across the world today groups of Christians meet. Jesus is there within each assembly no matter if the groups are large or small or even if they are meeting simultaneously. So, we see Jesus meets the first qualification identified above. He is omnipresent.

Second, Jesus' claim to omnipotence can be witnessed in John 29 when He states, "Destroy this temple, and in three days I will raise it up" (**John 2:19**). The resurrection of Jesus declares His all-powerful nature! He got up out of the grave. And for any reader who may doubt the resurrection, Paul explains there were around 500 witnesses who testified to seeing Jesus risen (**1 Cor. 15:3–11**). But more on this later.

Finally, witness to Jesus being omniscient is seen in Mark 2:8 where it is stated, "And immediately when Jesus perceived in his spirit that they so reasoned within themselves, he said unto them, Why reason ye these things in your hearts?" Jesus knows everything, including the secrets of our hearts. Jesus' claim of divinity is corroborated within each of the attributes considered above. Even more could be considered but space limits the discussion here.[73]

While each of the listed characteristics can be used to build the case attesting to Jesus' claim of Deity, for the sake of the present discussion, we need only remember the scope of miraculous events observed by the religious leaders of Jesus' day.

When considering Jesus' words and work as proof of His identity and supernatural origins, one might assume the Jewish leaders in His day were oblivious to the good things Jesus was doing, that maybe they were basing their criticisms of Him on unobserved rumor or maybe hearsay. But according to the gospel writers, this assumption isn't true. The religious leaders saw the evidence and simply refused to believe (**John 9:6**). Consider the account John records in his gospel, "Rabbi, we know that thou art a teacher come from God: for no man can do these miracles that thou doest, except God be with him" (**John 3.2**). The evidence that Jesus was on assignment from God was indeed in front of the religious leaders and by their own testimony they acknowledged the fact. Instead of embracing Jesus, they began to make up wild accusations concerning the works they beheld, even suggesting He was in league with the devil (**Matt. 12:24**). Not only can we witness the rejection of Jesus by the religious leaders within the Bible, but it is also possible to read of it in other historic sources outside of the Scriptures.

Generally speaking, the Talmud is a collection of Jewish teachings and opinions recorded by leading rabbis from about the time of Christ to the fifth century AD.[74] The topics addressed within its pages range from Jewish ethics to Jewish folklore. It is the primary source for Jewish religious law and theology even to this day. Observant Jews have looked to the collection over many centuries as a guide for daily conduct, and it is here where one source of extra-biblical evidence can be found which describes the rejection of Jesus by the religious leaders of His day.

There are two versions of the Jewish Talmud, the Jerusalem Talmud and the Babylonian Talmud. Just as their names suggest one work traces its origin to Jerusalem while the other traces its origin to Babylon which was a product of Judea's exile during the days of Daniel and Ezekiel. Within the Babylon version it is written "On the eve of the Passover they hanged Yeshu (Jesus) and the herald went before him for forty days saying he is going forth to be stoned in that he hath practiced sorcery and beguiled and led astray Israel."[75] Herein lies evidence from outside of the Bible within a revered Jewish holy book that the Jewish leaders saw the works of Jesus and yet still refused to acknowledged Him. This particular statement is accepted as being written during the first or second century AD.[76] It is considered as being written in close proximity to when the actual crucifixion of Christ occurred. The means the Talmudic writer himself may have had firsthand knowledge of the rejection by the religious leaders of Jesus.

Still further, there is other recorded testimony of Jesus' miracles from a historian of Jesus day, Flavius Josephus. Josephus writes in his *Antiquities of the Jews*, "About this time there lived Jesus, a wise man, (if indeed one ought to call him a man). For he was one who wrought surprising feats and was a teacher of such people as accept the truth gladly."[77] The material in parenthesis is thought to be suspect testimony attributed to Josephus which may have possibly been added later by a Christian editor.[78] Regardless of possible interpolation by an unidentified editor, the received testimony, minus that which may be suspect, of Josephus confirms Jesus as a miracle worker. Notice, Josephus describes these miracles as "surprising feats." Josephus was thought to have written in the latter half of the first century which means people were still talking about these miraculous feats that Jesus performed mere decades after His death.[79]

Within both biblical and non-biblical sources, it is clear Jesus is described as a miracle worker. These miraculous works unquestionably highlight something extraordinary about Jesus. At the very least, these works paint Jesus as no mere man. If the reports of His remarkable abilities are taken at face value, these works verify the claims Jesus and others made about His origins. Remember the blind man's testimony? "If this man were not of God, he could do nothing" (**John 9:33**).

It is intriguing to consider that God uses Luke, a doctor, to report on the birth story of Jesus. This doctor knew all about birth and what was involved with conceiving. This doctor knew all about the limitations which physically tether humanity. However, Doctor Luke knew there was something very different about Jesus. There was something which allowed Jesus to transcend the shared shackles of the race into which he was born. There was something otherworldly that seemed to explain Jesus' words and works. While this doctor would have been trained to view the world through the rational lens of science, Luke was convinced that the events he had witnessed concerning Jesus could not be explained by the mere laws of nature. He could only conclude that Jesus was something more than man. In Luke's mind, he believed that the difference could be explained in Jesus' birth account (**Luke 1:30–38**). A birth he describes as being instigated by God himself through his Holy Spirit who overshadowed a young girl named Mary impregnating her with divine seed.

In today's Western Culture, the stories which sell the most box office movie tickets are those who portray the works of superheroes. One popular superhero is a character known as Superman. The character was first brought to life in 1938 as a comic book release.[80] Since then, Superman has been depicted in countless comics, books, and movies. He is a character who has remarkable abilities such as flight, x-ray vision, and unmatched strength. The powers he possesses are not the result of some event or accident, they are the product of his origin story. Superman is depicted as coming from an alien world known as Krypton. Shortly before his home planet is destroyed, his parents place him in a ship which will take him to earth. Here, the child grows into an extraordinary individual who looks and acts like an average everyday person. But he possesses supernatural abilities that he employs for the good of humanity which are a product of his alien birth.

Does any part of this story sound familiar? To the reader of the Bible it should, as the story is very much like the story told of Jesus. The New Testament attributes Jesus' remarkable abilities to His origin story. Jesus comes to earth and grows into what is thought to be an ordinary individual but possesses extraordinary abilities—abilities used to help humanity as it struggles with overcoming the effects of a sin condition.

While the comparison of the fictional superhero Superman and Jesus Christ may be a stretch to some, it seems reasonable to consider that mankind has ever longed for someone to arrive on the scene to rescue it from the throws of evil which has trounced it from its initial fall into sin (Genesis 3). In the mind of some, such a hero can only be imagined within the pages of a tale only to be believed by the mind of a child. However within the pages of the greatest story ever told, found within the Bible, are the needs of an entire race corrected by a hero not wearing tights and a cape, but one who is wearing the tattered robe of a Jewish carpenter, a carpenter who will lay down his life as a ransom for the faces found within the race.

With the addressing of Jesus' miraculous words and ministry as proof of His supernatural origins, it is time now to move on to other evidence to which some would say is the most convincing for Christ's miraculous conception. The evidence which will be presented is the resurrection of Jesus. This next chapter will address the historical evidence for resurrection and the weight it offers in support of the virgin birth narrative.

9

Jesus' Resurrection

For I delivered unto you first of all that which I also received, how that Christ died for our sins according to the scriptures; And that he was buried, and that he rose again the third day according to the scriptures.
(1 Corinthians 15:3–4)

When considering the many miracles attributed to Jesus, none has come close to the lasting impact of the resurrection. This singular event has forever altered the course of human history in ways that those who witnessed the resurrected Christ could never imagine. Some seventeen centuries after Jesus' resurrection, Napoleon Bonaparte is credited with uttering, "I marvel that whereas the ambitious dreams of myself, Caesar, and Alexander should have vanished into thin air, a Judean peasant (Jesus) should be able to stretch His hands across the centuries and control the destinies of men and nations."[81] Napoleon's observation continues to ring true even today, some twenty-one centuries from the event.

Wars have been fought, nations established, kingdoms toppled, fortunes made and lost all because of this singular event in history. Even today, as many debate the direction of modern civilization, society's response to the resurrection proves to be the factor which ultimately determines its rise and/or fall. Consider the former Soviet Union for an example. The nation banned God from its society only to see the nation crumble some seventy years after its inception. Some attribute its fall to bad management.[82] No doubt godlessness leads to bad management (**Dan. 9:4–14**). If a nation acknowledges God, a belief in resurrection is not only possible but probable. This belief ultimately sets a course for success which will guide any nation and its activities because God will bless it (**Deut. 11:8**). If a nation refuses to acknowledge God, resurrection is not simply improbable but impossible. Likewise, this belief will ultimately set a course for failure which will ruin a nation and its activities, because God will curse it (**Deut. 11:16–17**). Truly, this is the conundrum which has plagued man for the last two thousand years, a juxtaposition where faith determines the success or failure of a nation.

As men today wrestle with the question of resurrection, it must be asked if there is historical support for the event. If the event can be pinpointed historically, a case can be made that supernatural intervention occurs just as Jesus represented (**Luke 4:16–27**). Specifically, if evidence of the Divine can be witnessed in the annuals of history through the event of the resurrection, there is no room to argue God's absence in the affairs of men. Scripture explains His intervention is solely responsible for the rise and fall of nations and peoples (**Job 12:23–25**). Acceptance of this event lends clear validation to the many episodes of intervention recorded within the Bible, including the virgin birth narrative of Jesus. But for now, focus should be placed on intervention as is seen in the historicity of resurrection which will in turn ultimately lend support for the miraculous conception thesis.

The Bible

The first source for credible evidence of resurrection comes from the Bible itself. Every New Testament writer either explicitly or implicitly references the resurrection event. This means that many of those who were closest to Jesus bore written, explicit witness to the historicity of His resurrection (**John 20; 1 Cor. 15:3–8**). But not everyone close to Jesus, referring to his biological brothers James and Jude, explicitly references the event in their writings. The brothers fail to directly attest to the claims of Jesus' resurrection in either of their credited accounts included in the New Testament. However, there seems to be ample implied belief by both within the manuscripts they present. For example, notice James refers to the "coming of the Lord" (**James 5:7**), as does Jude (**Jude 1:14**). If James or his brother had not witnessed the resurrected Christ, how could either believe Jesus would come again someday if He was still laying in the tomb? Most people realize that when someone dies, they should not set a place for them at the supper table. They are gone with no chance of return. However, James and Jude were both cogs in the wheel of the infant church.[83] They were very aware and largely responsible for what was being preached concerning their older brother (**Acts 15; Gal. 2**). If they objected to the message of Jesus' bodily resurrection, there is nothing witnessed within the writings of the pair nor is there testimony from other historical sources that record either of the two men at odds with the early church and its messaging.

Further, there is evidence the pair likely suffered mistreatment because of their commitment to the message of Jesus being preached. There is little doubt James, known as the just, suffered horrible mistreatment for his stand on the story of Jesus, including resurrection. The historical record describes him as being taken to the roof of the temple and there, cast off. Early historian Hegesippus writes that after landing on the ground with little life left within the leader of the Jerusalem church, James was bludgeoned to death by those who cast him down.[84] It is a little harder to ascertain what happened to Jude. Historical information regarding Jude is somewhat confusing as he is often confused with other figures surrounding Jesus and the early church. However, Eusebius notes that Jude's descendants were tried by Emperor Domitian and eventually martyred by Emperor Trajan. It can be concluded that if Jude's descendants were harassed and killed for their involvement with the early church, it is likely that Jude may have suffered the same fate as he too was influential in the early church as well.[85]

To endure such hard mistreatment would require great commitment to Christ and the events surrounding his life from those on the receiving end. It therefore seems very reasonable to suggest this pair of brothers was a great example of those willing to testify to the resurrection, and additionally to the virgin birth, of their brother Jesus.

The Nazareth Decree

A wonderful attestation of the historicity of the resurrection is seen in what is known as the Nazareth Decree. This somewhat small marble artifact was found in 1878 in the once hometown of Jesus in Nazareth.[86] Conservative biblical scholars believe it to have been produced between AD 41–54 coinciding with the reign of Emperor Claudius of Rome. Testimony from the inscription purports itself to be an "ordinance of Caesar." The writing style for the inscription seems to support the dating. The message written in Koine Greek, restricts anyone from removing a body from interment.[87]

It is my decision [concerning] graves and tombs—whoever has made them for the religious observances of parents, or children, or household members—that these remain undisturbed forever. But if anyone legally charges that another person has destroyed, or has in any manner extracted those who have been buried, or has moved with wicked intent those who have been buried to other places, committing a crime against them, or has moved sepulcher-sealing stones, against such a person, I order that a judicial tribunal be created, just as [is done] concerning the gods in human religious observances, even more so will it be obligatory to treat with honor those who have been entombed. You are absolutely not to allow anyone to move [those who have been entombed]. But if [someone does], I wish that [violator] to suffer capital punishment under the title of tomb-breaker.[88]

This decree might strike you as odd as some might see it as unnecessary given the fact that most graves usually go undisturbed. However, you should remember what was happening at this time. The degree was issued possibly less than ten years after Jesus' death and resurrection. The early church would have been preaching the resurrection of Jesus during this time (**Acts 12**). Witnesses such as Peter, Paul, John, and others were still alive, attesting what they had witnessed. Also, the Jewish leaders were still trying to snuff out the witnesses attesting to the resurrection. Remember, these leaders were the same ones who had initially floated the idea that Jesus' body was stolen by His disciples (**Matt. 28:13**).

Claudius, Roman emperor during this time, had probably been petitioned to pronounce the degree by some of the very same Jewish leaders who had been at the trial of Jesus and were responsible for His death (**Mark 14:53–65**). It is unlikely this decree was simply issued independently of the resurrection event as some have suggested.[89] Most laws, modern or ancient, are on the books because they are meant to address the behavior for which they was created. Likely, the resurrection account continued to gain popularity through the Roman Empire as the church was growing and the Jewish leaders wanted another piece of artillery to combat this growing Christian movement.

It is also noteworthy that Claudius expelled the Jews from Rome around this period of time.[90] This seems to have been due to the many riots which the Jews had been guilty of instigating. Many riots stemmed from the response the gospel was receiving by those Jews in various cities throughout the empire (**Acts 21:27–36**). This response to evangelism may have gotten the emperor's attention and the degree was his way of shutting down the story Christians were telling.

This discovery of the Nazareth decree is probably the greatest archeological evidence found to date supporting the historicity of resurrection from antiquity. To find this degree proves there indeed was pushback from the Roman authorities to the message of Christ's resurrection being preached by the early Christians. It further proves that the biblical narrative found in the gospels and in Acts is reliable. It lends credibility to the assertion that Luke and the other writers were faithfully recording what they had seen and witnessed. It is only reasonable to assume the other elements concerning the life of Jesus and the church as recorded were probably based in truth as well, the chief of which outside of resurrection is virgin birth.

Tacitus

Publius Cornelius Tacitus is a renowned Roman historian who lived in the mid- to late first and early second centuries. He is credited with detailing most of the goings-on of the empire in his two volumes of work, *the Annals* and *the Histories*.[91] Between the two works, Tacitus is thought to have written approximately thirty volumes filled with a trove of details which were the most relevant within the empire. Among the topics, Tacitus references Christ. Further, he writes concerning a peculiarity held by Christ's followers.

"Christus, from whom the name had its origin, suffered the extreme penalty during the reign of Tiberius at the hand of one of our procurators, Pontius Pilatus, and a most mischievous superstition, thus checked for the moment, again broke out not only in Judea, the first source of the evil, but even in Rome." [92]

While Tacitus writes more concerning the Christians of his day, the reference above is all that will be examined in this discussion. From Tacitus, we learn several important facts in regards to the subject of resurrection. First, Christ is identified as a historical figure. Second, Christians were named after their founder. Next, Christ was put to death by Pontius Pilatus during the reign of Tiberius. Then, a superstition broke out concerning Christ in Judea. Finally, the followers of Christ carried the superstition to Rome.

To those who question the life of Jesus, here is historical evidence from outside the Bible that Jesus really lived. While there is other evidence of Jesus from antiquity, attention must be turned to Tacitus' report for the sake of this discussion.

Tacitus explains that something happened in regards to the death of Christus. He references the event as a "mischievous superstition."[93] There is little doubt Tacitus is referencing the events surrounding the reports of Jesus' resurrection. When individuals die that is usually the end of their story. However, Tacitus explains something more was being reported concerning the end of Jesus. The report was responsible for sweeping through Judea and causing a stir among its citizenry.

Tacitus' report seems to align perfectly with what is chronicled by Luke in his gospel and in the Acts. However, Luke provides an eyewitness account of the events with greater detail provided than Tacitus. Tacitus says the superstition was carried all the way to Rome from the back waters of Judea. Luke concurs saying the disciples of Christ were responsible for the report being preached in Rome (**Acts 28:1–31**).

It appears the historicity of Jesus' resurrection is supported from antiquity. The reason it is important to establish the historical support for resurrection is to show that the record of the biblical text is based in truth. If resurrection can be established as an historical event, then subjects like the virgin birth can also be argued to have been based in historical truth. If resurrection was a real event, it seems ever more logical that miraculous conception is true. I feel the two occurrences are inseparable, being the two sides of the same coin. One event is dependent upon the other. But, before the subject of historical support for the resurrection is put to bed, attention should be given to another historian who was a little closer in proximity to the events which surrounded it.

Josephus

Flavius Josephus was a Jewish historian who lived contemporaneously with many of the events which are recorded in the New Testament. He is best known for his two works *The Jewish War* and the *Antiquities of the Jews*, both written in the latter half of the first century. While Josephus was Jewish by birth, he spent much of his career in the service of the Roman Empire, at one point serving as a court historian for emperor Vespasian.[94]

Josephus chronicled many of the events occurring in Palestine during the first century. The subjects he covers include the Roman sacking of Jerusalem in AD 70 after the Jewish revolt and the Roman conquest of Masada from AD 73–74. His testimony has also unwittingly provided secular support for many events reported by New Testament writers, chief of which is Jesus' resurrection.[95]

Josephus records an interesting account of Jesus known today as the *Testimonium Flavianum*. In this account, Josephus seems to acknowledge many of the biographical facts concerning Jesus which were being communicated by the early church, notably His ministry, His death at the hands of Pilate, and subsequent resurrection three days later. While many scholars take exception to the discourse as probably being redacted by a later Christian editor, it seems most believe the fundamental facts cited are likely part of an authentic account chronicled by Josephus.[96] The account reads as follows:

> About this time there lived Jesus, a wise man, if indeed one ought to call him a man. For he was one who performed surprising deeds and was a teacher of such people as accept the truth gladly.

He won over many Jews and many of the Greeks. He was the Christ. And when, upon the accusation of the principal men among us, Pilate had condemned him to a cross, those who had first come to love him did not cease. He appeared to them spending a third day restored to life, for the prophets of God had foretold these things and a thousand other marvels about him. And the tribe of the Christians, so called after him, has still to this day not disappeared.[97]

Some of the testimony concerning Jesus quoted by Josephus may seem a bit exaggerated. This is especially true if Josephus is not a Christian. The second century historian, Origen of Alexandria describes Josephus as not a believer of Jesus as the Christ. However, Josephus' testimony is striking as it corroborates what was being preached concerning Jesus even at this early date in the latter half of the first century.[98] The topic which takes top billing in Josephus' account is Jesus' resurrection appearance on the third day restored to life.[99]

Even stripped of what sounds to be of Christian influence, the report is staggering. Consider how revolutionary this description would have been coming from this non-believer. We have Josephus reporting what is being said of Christ within a generation of when His resurrection is alleged to have occurred. What's more is that he reports "the tribe of the Christians, so called after him, has still to this day not disappeared."[100] This means that the death of Christ did not snuff out the movement He started. From the resurrection forward there are conversions occurring even in the face of bloody persecution. What is responsible for the sudden explosion of converts to Christianity? Resurrection.

Resurrection affirms that God placed His stamp of validation on the life and message of Jesus. God could have left Jesus to rot in the grave if what Jesus preached was not approved by God, but He did not (**Acts 2:22–24**). Further, after God raised Jesus, the Holy Spirit began to transform the lives of thousands who would come to trust Jesus as Savior. While apparently not a believer, Josephus is providing testimony to what he witnessed as a result of the event of Jesus' resurrection.

Why is it important to be convinced of Jesus' resurrection? It is important because if resurrection is factual, the miraculous conception or virgin birth account of Jesus' origin is likely factual as well. If Jesus could get up after being dead three days, obviously there was something very different about this man. If resurrection can be validated by historical eyewitness testimony, it would seem the virgin birth origin account is all the more plausible.

No human could logically testify to the accuracy of the miraculous conception event except Mary, which she did. However, resurrection could easily have been attested by witnesses. Paul explains that the majority of some 500 people could provide eyewitness testimony to

Jesus' bodily resurrection (**1 Cor. 15:3**). Paul's statement explains that there were some within that number who were then deceased but the majority were available for questioning and were willing to talk.

In a court of law, it is possible to convict a defendant with the testimony provided by one witness. But in the case of Christ's resurrection, Paul is convinced that hundreds which he refers to the Corinthian church could provide testimony to seeing Jesus alive after being raised on the third day after His crucifixion. It is therefore concluded that the magnitude of eyewitness testimony cited by Paul more than meets the threshold requirements necessary to have the event legally verified in any modern court proceeding.

10

Conclusion

Through faith we understand that the worlds were framed by the word of God, so that things which are seen were not made of things which do appear.
(Hebrews 11:3)

Those who argue against virgin birth, or miraculous conception, argue from the point of naturalistic observation.[101] This is to say they doubt virgin birth because this is not what can be observed in nature among humans today. This persuasion is very much like the scientific doubt placed upon the young earth theory which says that which is observed today in nature is what has always been at work in nature. These theorists deny God's direct intervention which could have, or can at any time, changed the processes which are observed. This is known as uniformitarianism.[102]

It should be remembered that anyone who hopes to be taken seriously by the world of secular academia is forced to color within the ridged lines of the authorized scientific construct formulated from the inductive reasoning offered by Francis Bacon in the sixteenth century.[103] While employing the scientific method to record or test what is witnessed in the natural world provides a wonderful tool for discovery, it should be remembered this tool only reflects what is occurring at any given moment in time. The scientific method in itself is not a rule by which the universe is governed. It is simply a way to measure or record what is happening at any given moment.

It was the German-born physicist Albert Einstein who cemented the importance of incorporating the element of time along with the three dimensions of space into the manifold of scientific observation.[104] The reason for its importance is evident in that circumstances and factors can change at any given moment. It can be postulated that because conditions are favorable for beautiful weather to be observed today doesn't mean the same conditions existed yesterday or will exist tomorrow. There are factors which influence weather patterns which result in varying conditions from day to day. It is these anomalies which have to be factored if one is to provide an accurate model for observing weather patterns.

As outside influence is acknowledged in the weather model just discussed, the same willingness to acknowledge external influences must be considered when providing a working model of the creation as we know it. Science likes to define the observable creation as a closed system, which simply means the observable patterns at play have always been and will always continue to be as they are today. However, this model does not work even when considering what is observable today. The law of entropy dictates everything is running toward an inevitable end. Entropy can have a large impact on the sustainability of the processes at work in nature at any given time.

Consider the eruption of Mount Saint Helens in Washington State in 1980.[105] This eruption was the catalyst for many phenomena which were observable during the hours and days immediately following the blast which are unseen today. The largest landslide in recorded history was witnessed, glaciers melted in moments, and mudslides wiped out acres of old-growth forests in seconds. This devastation left the mountain along with miles surrounding it scarred for decades. This singular event disrupted the natural processes which had defined this area for centuries in mere moments. Other such disruptions can be cited such as the supposed meteor which took out the dinosaurs 65 million years ago, the Chelyabinsk Meteor, which exploded over Russia in 1908 leaving hundreds injured, and the Minoan Eruption which devastated the island of Thera in 1600 BC. All of these events disrupted natural systems observable at their given times in history.

The reason each of these events is cited is to demonstrate that the belief that natural processes can never be interrupted is ridiculous. For the uniformitarianists to ardently hold this position, insisting that natural processes can never be changed, is clearly undefendable. The examples cited in the preceding paragraph are anomalies which have left enormous impacts on the world. If such anomalies have interrupted the natural processes governing the terrestrial world, then one can rightly extrapolate that interruptions may be more common than we think, even that these interruptions could be the divine intent of a God who is orchestrating events according to a plan He long ago determined.

Now, before you dismiss the idea just stated, consider that if God is responsible for the entirety of creation, all the universe and any multiverses identified in modern physics, He as God has the ability to act upon His creation as He sees fit. He is God, which means He is omnipresent, omniscient, and omnipotent. It would mean He is not governed by the same laws of physics which govern His creation. He exists outside of this creation. It means He is able to move in and out of time. Remember, time is a construct of this creation. He would be able to move and to do at His discretion, which leads us back to the miraculous conception or virgin birth event.

We should not be surprised that God can choose to enter into our plain of existence through a stable in Bethlehem. He is God remember? He can do anything.

Conclusion

What should surprise us is that He would choose to enter our plain of existence at all. But nevertheless, Paul records that at just the right time He came to earth to set right what had been broken through the fall of Adam (**Gal. 4:4**).

In the foregoing pages, evidence for the virgin birth has been given. Based on the evidence provided, I am convinced that this miraculous conception event is an actual historical happening. But beyond being convinced of the historical event, you should ask yourself why. Why, at just the right time, did God chose to send His son? While we may grapple with the details and proofs surrounding the event, the answer as to why God sent His son is easy to ascertain. "For God so loved the world" is arguably the most profound, yet simple statement men will ever consider (**John 3:16**). God is crazy in love with His creation, which means He is crazy in love with you and me.

To the scholar critical of this love affair, the idea of a supreme God feeling anything but contempt for a creation which has mocked and doubted His very existence and has laughed away His instructions is unthinkable. Over the years, I have created many works which were discarded for one flaw or another, but the flaws were never as contemptible as those which have been leveled toward God by His own creation. One would think God would simply discard this messed up creation and start over, but that is not what God has chosen to do. Love is His motivator.

Going back to John 3:16, you need to pay close attention to the smallest word included within this declaration, the word *so*. It is translated from the Greek word *houtōs*. For our purposes, it has a couple of different meanings. First, the word can refer to extent. This is how most English readers understand what's being said in the statement. The word is used as an adverb to modify the verb love, as is read in the King James Version. God didn't just love His creation, he "so" loved His creation. Meaning His love was magnified or deep. But it seems the statement is actually using the word *houtōs* in a different way. When the statement is read from the Greek, the meaning is understood to refer to what God did because of His love for His creation. God loved and this is what He did because He loved. Therefore, the translated statement is more accurately translated as "For this is how God loved the world." What did He do? He sent His one and only Son, Jesus.

Jesus is the solution to the problem facing the creation. He died to take care of the problem of sin. Sin is the root to every problem man faces in this life. Whether the problem is spiritual, medical, or whatever, it can always be traced back to sin. While sin still eats away at this creation, Jesus' atoning death redeems mankind and makes him fit for eternity as God intended him to be. One day Jesus will return to this earth to set right all that sin has mired.

While this work has focused on arguments for virgin birth, we have to ultimately understand why such a birth was necessary. Sin had to be dealt with and the only sacrifice which could atone for it had to be without the stain of sin. Jesus, born of Mary without the seed of a human father, was free from the curse of sin because it is surmised that sin is transferred through the human father. He was perfect, blemish free. Jesus' sinless perfection made Him the only sacrifice which could bring a lasting remedy for the effects of sin upon creation.

Years ago, I attended a class taught by noted Bible professor Dr. John C. Whitcomb. Dr. Whitcomb brought to light a wonderful interpretation of Hebrews 11:3 which has stayed with me. In the class, Dr. Whitcomb stated that it is only through the faith relationship with God that men can begin to understand the truths of how and why God has intervened within this material world. This idea is simply profound. I maintain that no amount of study will enable men to discover truth without the divine revelation of God. Make no mistake, study and preparation are important, but without God men are destined to make assumptions and to offer analysis which, more often than not, do not align with truth. This teaching aligns with Jesus' statement in John 14:26 when He explains, "But the Comforter, who is the Holy Ghost whom the Father will send in my name, he shall teach you all things." Not only does God illuminate the mind of the minister as he proclaims his sermon to his congregation but likewise, He illuminates the minds of the astronomer, the medical doctor, and the engineer, to come to correct interpretations of truth.

Unfortunately today, many believe they can arrive at untarnished truth without God. In fact, many believe the only way to discover truth is to reject God outright. They believe mistakenly that God only wants to confuse and undermine objective truth. But to reject God is to simply reap the winds of disaster. Consider modern America, the nation suffers from confusion of gender identity, confusion regarding race relations, confusion regarding the necessity of parental responsibility, and the list goes on. The reason for this confusion is the rejection of God by so many. The prophet Daniel repented of Judah's rejection of God during the nation's captivity in Babylon. Daniel pointed to the same confusion displayed by Judah as proof of the nation's rebellion toward God (**Dan. 9:5–7**). Daniel concludes Judah received what it deserved by way of captivity because of its wicked abandonment of God. One wonders how long God will allow America to continue down this path before judgement will inevitably cripple the nation.

The writer of Hebrews provides the answer to the problem of interpretation of thought. It is only through the relationship of faith, between God and man, that a correct understanding of truth can be achieved.

Finally, the writer of Hebrews leaves us with one last admonition to apply to this work. Hebrews 12 states, "Wherefore seeing we also are compassed about with so great a cloud of witnesses, let us lay aside every weight, and the sin which doth so easily beset *us*, and let us run with patience the race that is set before us" (**Heb. 12:1**).

An examination of prophetic declaration combined with eyewitness testimony has been employed in the consideration of the miraculous conception event. Given the strength outlined without this work of evidence in support of the event, it is my hope that you will be left with the opinion that this blessed event is in fact true without a shadow of a doubt. If you remain unconvinced, I hope that the work will, if nothing else, challenge you to begin your own investigation into the subject.

Lastly to the reader, thank you for your willingness to consider the material in this work. If you are a Christian, it is my hope that your walk with Christ will be strengthened from the study presented here. If you are lost, please consider the testimony here and let it encourage you to make Christ Savior and Lord of your life. Remember, the greatest proof of God's intervention into this creation is the changed lives which have been left in the wake of the gospel message. God can forever change your life today if you are willing. Thank you for your time and willingness to consider my arguments and conclusions.

About the Author

Richard Larry Brooks, II. serves as pastor of New Harvest Missionary Baptist Church in LaFayette, Georgia. Pastor Brooks is a graduate of Liberty University where he received a Master of Arts Degree in Management and Leadership. He is also a graduate of Temple Baptist Seminary (now Piedmont Divinity School) where he graduated as Salutatorian with a Master of Arts Degree in Biblical Studies. Brooks has served in pastorate roles for over twenty-five years. He and his wife, Leigh, call North Georgia home. They have two adult children, Ally and Logan.

Endnotes

1 Nell Rose. "Was Jesus' Father Really a Roman Soldier Named Tiberius Pantera?" HubPages. July 12, 2015. https://discover.hubpages.com/religion-philosophy/Who-Was-Jesuss-Real-Father-and-What-Is-The-Panthera-Connection.

2 Liam Stack. "How the 'War on Christmas' Controversy Was Created." The New York Times. December 19, 2016. https://www.nytimes.com/2016/12/19/us/war-on-christmas-controversy.html.

3 Tony Burke. "Christmas Stories in Christian Apocrypha." Bible History Daily. December 19, 2018. Biblical Archaeology Society. https://www.biblicalarchaeology.org/daily/biblical-topics/bible-interpretation/christmas-stories-in-christian-apocrypha/.

4 Mary Eberstadt. "Regular Christians Are No Longer Welcome in American Culture." *Time* magazine. June 26, 2016. https://time.com/4385755/faith-in-america/

5 Valerie Tarico. "11 Kinds of Bible Verses Christians Love to ignore." Salon. May 31, 2014. https://www.salon.com/2014/05/31/11_kinds_of_bible_verses_christians_love_to_ignore_partner/.

6   Terry Gross. "If Jesus Never Called Himself God, How Did He Become One?" National Public Radio. April 7, 2014. https://www.npr.org/2014/04/07/300246095/if-jesus-never-called-himself-god-how-did-he-become-one.

7   John Blake. "Decoding Jesus: Separating Man from Myth." CNN. March 7, 2017. https://www.cnn.com/2017/02/15/living/jesus-debate-man-versus-myth/index.html.

8   Bart Ehrman. "Why Would I Call Myself Both an Agnostic or an Atheist? A Blast from the Past." The Bart Ehrman Blog: The History and Literature of Early Christianity. The Bart Ehrman Foundation. July 4, 2017. https:// ehrmanblog.org/am-i-an-agnostic-or-an-atheist-a-blast-from- the-past/.

9   Brian Leiter. "Moral Skepticism and Moral Disagreement: Developing an Argument from Nietzsche." On the Human. March 25, 2010. https://nationalhumanitiescenter.org/on-the-human/2010/03/moral-skepticism-and-moral-disagreement-developing-an-argument-from-nietzsche/.

10 "Entropy," Wikipedia, last modified March 23, 2022, https://en.wikipedia.org/wiki/Entropy.

11 Efraim Goldstein. "Almah: Virgin or Young Maiden?" One For Israel. 2009. https://www.oneforisrael.org/bible-based-teaching-from-israel/isaiah-714-virgins-birth/.

12 Bart Ehrman. "Why Was Jesus Born of a Virgin in Matthew and Luke?" The Bart Herman

Blog: The History and Literature of Early Christianity. The Bart Ehrman Foundation. December 24, 2014. https://ehrmanblog.org/why-was-jesus-born-of-a-virgin-in-matthew-and-luke/.

13 N. N. Trakakis. "Why I Am Not Orthodox." ABC. December 7, 2015. New York City. https://www.abc.net.au/religion/why-i-am-not-orthodox/10097536.

14 "The Great Isaiah Scroll." The Digital Dead Sea Scrolls. http://dss.collections.imj.org.il/isaiah.

15 "Isaiah Scroll," *W*ikipedia, last modified January 29, 2022. https://en.wikipedia.org/wiki/Isaiah_Scroll.

16 Christopher Eames. "The Antiquity of the Scriptures: The Prophets." Watch Jerusalem. November 25, 2017. https://watchjerusalem.co.il/21-the-antiquity-of-the-scriptures-the-prophets.

17 Jeff A. Benner. "The Great Isaiah Scroll and the Masoretic Text." The Ancient Hebrew Research Center. https://www.ancient-hebrew.org/dss/great-isaiah-scroll-and-the-masoretic-text.htm.

18 John R. Kohlenberger, III. and William D. Mounce, Editors. "Alma." Kohlenberger/Mounce Concise Hebrew-Aramaic Dictionary of the Old Testament. OakTree Software, Inc. Version 3.3. 2012

19 "Septuagint," Wikipedia, last modified March 18, 2022, https://en.wikipedia.org/wiki/Septuagint.

20 "Septuagint," Wikipedia, last modified March 18, 2022, https://en.wikipedia.org/wiki/Septuagint.

21 Paul Koreen. "Did Jesus Actually Read from the Septuagint?" Quora. April 21, 2017. https://www.quora.com/Did-Jesus-Christ-actually-read-from-the-Septuagint.

22 Joseph Thayer. Editor. *"parthenos."* Thayer's English-Greek Lexicon of the New Testament. Oaktree Software, Inc. Version 1.7.

23 "Septuagint," Wikipedia, last modified March 18, 2022, https://en.wikipedia.org/wiki/Septuagint.

24 "Protevangelium," Wikipedia, last modified February 11, 2022, https://en.wikipedia.org/wiki/Protevangelium.

25 David Rohl. *Legend: The Genesis of Civilization.* (United Kingdom: Century, 1998), 16.

26 John Davis. *Paradise to Prison.* (Grand Rapids, Michigan: Baker Book House, 1975), 91.

27 David Aaron. "Shedding Light on God's Body," The Harvard Theological Review, Vol. 90, No. 3 (July 1997), 299–314.

28 D. Blair Smith. "How Did Jesus Do Miracles—His Divine Nature or the Holy Spirit?" The Gospel Coalition. January 14, 2020. https://www.thegospelcoalition.org/article/jesus-miracles-who-how/.

29 "First Book of Adam and Eve." In *The Lost Books of the Bible and the Forgotten Books of Eden.* (Cleveland, OH: World Bible Publishers, Inc), 3–59.

30 Charles Darwin. *On the Origin of Species by Means of Natural Selection, or, The Preservation of Favoured Races in the Struggle for Life.* (London: J. Murray, 1859), 5.

31 Gary Habermas. *The Historical Jesus, Ancient Evidence for the Life of Christ.* (Joplin, Missouri: College Press Publishing Company, 1996), 153.

32 "Gamaliel," Wikipedia, last modified March 4, 2022, https://en.wikipedia.org/wiki/Gamaliel.

33 Josh McDowell. *The New Evidence that Demands a Verdict.* (Nashville: Thomas Nelson Publishers, 1999), 124–125.

34 Joseph Thayer. "*historeō*." Thayer's English-Greek Lexicon of the New Testament. Oaktree Software, Inc. Version 1.7.

35 Joseph Thayer. "*ginomai*." Thayer's English-Greek Lexicon of the New Testament. Oaktree Software, Inc. Version 1.7.

36 Glen Andrews Peoples. "St. Paul Quoted the Gospel of Luke." The Blog of Doctor Glenn Andrews Peoples on Theology, Philosophy, and Social Issues. Right Reason. January 24, 2015. http://www.rightreason.org/2015/paul-quoted-luke/.

37 Randy Ingermanson. "James, the Brother of Jesus, Part 1." Randy Ingermanson. February 28, 2019. https://www.ingermanson.com/james-brother-jesus/.

38 "Paul Meets Peter and James." Ligonier. January 13, 2009. https://www.ligonier.org/learn/devotionals/paul-meets-peter-and-james

39 Hershel Shanks and Ben Witherington, III. *The Bother of Jesus.* (New York: HarperOne, 2003), 23–26.

40 Aharei Mot Kedoshim. "Caring for Our Parents." Jewish Theological Seminary. May 9, 2009. https://www.jtsa.edu/torah/caring-for-our-parents/.

41 "Unknown Years of Jesus," Wikipedia, last modified February 18, 2022, https://en.wikipedia.org/wiki/Unknown_years_of_Jesus.

42 James Strong. "*tekton*." Strong's Greek Dictionary of the New Testament. Public Domain. Formatted and hypertext by OakTree Software, Inc. Version 2.8.

43 Eusebius of Caesarea. *The History of the Church.* (Grand Rapids, Michigan: Wm. B. Eerdmans Publishing Company, 2019), 128.

44 "Desposyni," Religion Wiki, retrieved February 16, 2022, https://religion.fandom.com/wiki/Desposyni.

45 James Strong. "*delphus*." Strong's Greek Dictionary of the New Testament. Public Domain. Formatted and hypertext by OakTree Software, Inc. Version 2.8.

Endnotes

46 Clement of Alexandria. *Adumbrations: Ancient Christian Commentary*. (Westmont, Illinois: InterVarsity Press, 2000), 245.

47 Warner J. Wallace. "Is Mark's Gospel an Early Memoir of the Apostle Peter?" Cold Case Christianity. July 25, 2018. https://coldcasechristianity.com/writings/is-marks-gospel-an-early-memoir-of-the-apostle-peter/.

48 James Strong. *"delphos."* Strong's Greek Dictionary of the New Testament. Public Domain. Formatted and hypertext by OakTree Software, Inc. Version 2.8.

49 Vivan Bricker. "Do We Know How Old Mary was When She Had Jesus?" Christianity.com. December 3, 2021. https://www.christianity.com/wiki/holidays/do-we-know-how-old-mary-was-when-she-had-jesus.html.

50 Dan Delzell. "Does the Book of James Promote Salvation by Works?" The Christian Post. November 9, 2021. https://www.christianpost.com/voices/does-the-book-of-james-promote-salvation-by-works.html.

51 Amanda Kolson Hurley. "The Last Days of James." Biblical Archaeology Society Online Archive. November/December 2002. https://www.baslibrary.org/biblical-archaeology-review/28/6/14.

52 Amanda Kolson Hurley. "The Last Days of James." Biblical Archaeology Society Online Archive.

November/December 2002. https://www.baslibrary.org/biblical-archaeology-review/28/6/14.

53 Erik Manning. "13 Good Historical Reasons for the Early Dating of the Gospels." Is Jesus Alive? December 19, 2019. https://isjesusalive.com/13-good-historical-reasons-for-the-early-dating-of-the-gospels/

54 "Seventy Disciples," Wikipedia, January 9, 2022, https://en.wikipedia.org/wiki/Seventy_disciples.

55 Norman Geisler and William Nix. *A General Introduction to the Bible.* (Chicago: Moody Press, 1986), 215.

56 Gary Habermas. *The Historical Jesus.* (Joplin, Missouri: College Press, 2001), 143–170.

57 Harold L. Willmington. *Willmington's Bible Handbook.* (Wheaton, Illinois: Tyndale House Publishers, 1997), 677.

58 Austin Cline. "When was the Gospel According to Mark Written?" Learn Religions. August 31, 2020. https://www.learnreligions.com/gospel-according-to-mark-248660.

59 E. P. Sanders. "St. Paul the Apostle." *Encyclopedia Britannica Online.* https://www.britannica.com/biography/Saint-Paul-the-Apostle.

60 Norman Geisler. "The Dating of the New Testament." Bethinking. 2022.

https://www.bethinking.org/bible/the-dating-of-the-new-testament.

61 Eusebius of Caesarea. *The History of the Church.* (Grand Rapids, Michigan: Wm. B. Eerdmans Publishing Company, 2019), 79.

62 Marvin W. Meyer. *The Gospel of Thomas: The Hidden Sayings of Jesus.* (New York: HarperCollins Publishers, 2004), 8.

63 "Mary, Mother of Jesus," Wikipedia, last modified March 23, 2022, https://en.wikipedia.org wikiMary,_mother_of_Jesus#cite_note-75.

64 Margaret Manning Shull. "Credible Witnesses." RZIM. https://www.rzim.org/read/a-slice-of-infinity/credible-witnesses.

65 Origen of Alexandria. Henry Chadwick, editor. *Contra Celsum.* (Cambridge: Cambridge University Press, 1980), 31.

66 Patrick Henry Reardon. "Mary at the Cross." *Christianity Today.* https://www.christianitytoday.com/history/issues/issue-83/mary-at-cross.html.

67 "Mary, Did You Know?," Wikipedia, last modified March 22, 2022, https://en.wikipedia.org/w/index.php?title=Mary,_Did_You_Know%3F&action=history.

68 Paul Maier. "Josephus the Essential Writings." (Grand Rapids: Kregel Publications, 1988), 264.

69 Joseph Thayer. "*kuros*." Thayer's English-Greek Lexicon of the New Testament. Oaktree Software, Inc. Version 1.7.

70 Joseph Thayer. "*proskuno*." Thayer's English-Greek Lexicon of the New Testament. Oaktree Software, Inc. Version 1.7.

71 The Anchor Bible Dictionary, George Howard. Volume 6. (New York: Anchor Bible, 1992) "The Tetragram and the New Testament."

72 "The Origins of the Septuagint." Associates for Biblical Research. https://biblearchaeology.org/research/new-testament-era/4022-a-brief-history-of-the-septuagint.

73 Harold Willmington. *Willmington's Bible Handbook.* (Wheaton, Illinois: Tyndale House Publishers, 1997), 614.

74 "Talmud." The Eerdmans Bible Dictionary. (Grand Rapids, Michigan: Wm. B. Eerdmans Publishing Company, 1987), 982.

75 Gary R. Habermas. *Ancient Evidence for the Life of Jesus.* (Nashville: Thomas Nelson Publishers, 1984), 98.

76 Gary R. Habermas. *Ancient Evidence for the Life of Jesus.* (Nashville: Thomas Nelson Publishers, 1984), 98.

77 Paul L. Maier. *Josephus The Essential Writings.* (Grand Rapids: Michigan: Kregel Publications, 1988), 264.

78 Paul L. Maier. *Josephus The Essential Writings.* (Grand Rapids: Michigan: Kregel Publications, 1988), 12.

79 Paul L. Maier. *Josephus The Essential Writings.* (Grand Rapids: Michigan: Kregel Publications, 1988), 12.

80 "Superman," Wikipedia, last modified April 3, 2022, https://en.wikipedia.org/wiki/Superman.

81 "Everything in Him Astonishes Me." The Blog. 2017. Here Comes the Sun. http://herecomestheson.net/2018/02/everything-in-him-astonishes me#:~:text=%E2%80%9CI%20marvel%20that%20whereas%20the,destinies%20of%20men%20and%20nations.%E2%80%9D.

82 Janos, Adam. "Was the Soviet Union's Collapse Inevitable?" April 17, 2018. History. https://www.history.com/news/why-did-soviet-union-fall.

83 Eusebius of Caesarea. "Eusebius and the Early Church." January 28, 2010. CSUN. https://www.csun.edu/~hcfll004/euseb_ch.html.

84 "The Unsettling Truth of James' Martyred Death." April 6, 2019. Steppes of Faith. https://medium.com/@steppesoffaith_56895/the-unsettling-truth-of-james-martyred-death-f677b9aa2c03.

85 "Jude, brother of Jesus." Wikipedia, last modified March 4, 2022, https://en.wikipedia.org/wiki/Jude,_brother_of_Jesus#:~:text=Jude%20

(alternatively%20Judas%20or%20Judah,according%20to%20the%20New%20Testament.

86 "Nazareth Inscription." Wikipedia, last modified January 8, 2022, https://en.wikipedia.org/wiki/Nazareth_Inscription.

87 "The Shiloh Excavations." January 1, 2021. Associates for Biblical Research. https://biblearchaeology.org/research/new-testament-era/2857-the-nazareth-inscription-proof-of-the-resurrection-of-christ-part-i.

88 "Nazareth Inscription," Wikipedia, last modified January 8, 2022, https://en.wikipedia.org/wiki/Nazareth_Inscription.

89 Mindy Wiseberger. "Was the 'Nazareth Inscription' a Roman response to Jesus' empty tomb? New evidence says it wasn't." April 17, 2020. LiveScience. https://www.livescience.com/nazareth-inscription-jesus-tomb-reinterpreted.html.

90 Mark Galli. "Persecution in the Early Church: A Gallery of the Persecuting Emperors." January/February 2022. Christianity Today. https://www.christianitytoday.com/history/issues/issue-27/persecution-in-early-church-gallery-of-persecuting-emperors.html.

91 "Tacitus," Wikipedia, last modified March 22 2022, https://en.wikipedia.org/wiki/Tacitus.

92 Gary Habermas. *Ancient Evidence for the Life of Jesus.* (Nashville: Thomas Nelson Publishers, 1984) 87–88.

93 Gary Habermas. *Ancient Evidence for the Life of Jesus.* (Nashville: Thomas Nelson Publishers, 1984) 89.

94 "Josephus." Wikipedia, last modified April 3, 2022, https://en.wikipedia.org/wiki/Josephus.

95 Paul Maier. *Josephus the Essential Writings.* (Grand Rapids: Kregel Publications, 1988) 264–265.

96 "Josephus on Jesus." Wikipedia, last modified March 31 2022, https://en.wikipedia.org/wiki/Josephus_on_Jesus .

97 Paul Maier. *Josephus the Essential Writings.* (Grand Rapids: Kregel Publications. 1988) 264–265.

98 "Ante-Nicene Fathers/Volume IX/Origen on Matthew/Origen's Commentary on Matthew/Book X/Chapter 17." Wikipedia, last modified July 31, 2021, https://en.wikisource.org/wiki/Ante-Nicene_Fathers/Volume_IX/Origen_on_Matthew/Origen%27s_Commentary_on_Matthew/Book_X/Chapter_17

99 Paul Maier. "Josephus the Essential Writings." (Grand Rapids: Kregel Publications, 1988), 264.

100 Paul Maier. "Josephus the Essential Writings." (Grand Rapids: Kregel Publications, 1988), 265.

101 R. Goodvin & B. A. Sarb. "Social Development (Attachment, Imprinting)." 2012. ScienceDirect. https://www.sciencedirect.com/topics/psychology/naturalistic-observation.

102 "Uniformitarianism." Wikipedia, last modified April 1, 2022, https://en.wikipedia.org/wiki/Uniformitarianism.

103 "History of the Scientific Method." Wikipedia, last modified March 30, 2022. https://en.wikipedia.org/wiki/History_of_scientific_method.

104 "Spacetime." Wikipedia, last modified April 10, 2022, https://en.wikipedia.org/wiki Spacetime#:~:text=In%20physics%2C%20space-time%20is%20any,a%20single%20four%2D-dimensional%20manifold.&text=The%20physicist%20Albert%20Einstein%20helped,of%20his%20theory%20of%20relativity.

105 "1980 Eruption of Mount St. Helens." Wikipedia, last modified April 8, 2022. https://en.wikipedia.org/wiki/1980_eruption_of_Mount_St._Helens.